The Open University

Investigating the Social World 1

Edited by Karim Murji

This publication forms part of the Open University module DD103 *Investigating the social world*. Details of this and other Open University modules can be obtained from Student Recruitment, The Open University, PO Box 197, Milton Keynes MK7 6BJ, United Kingdom (tel. +44 (0)300 303 5303; email general-enquiries@open.ac.uk).

Alternatively, you may visit the Open University website at www.open.ac.uk where you can learn more about the wide range of modules and packs offered at all levels by The Open University. To purchase a selection of Open University materials visit www.ouw.co.uk, or contact Open University Worldwide, Walton Hall, Milton Keynes MK7 6AA, United Kingdom for a brochure (tel. +44 (0)1908 858793; fax +44 (0)1908 858787; email ouw-customer-services@open.ac.uk).

The Open University, Walton Hall, Milton Keynes MK7 6AA

First published 2015

Edited, designed and typeset by The Open University.

Printed in the United Kingdom by Bell & Bain Ltd, Glasgow.

ISBN 978 178 00 7955 4

1.1

Investigating the Social World 1

Contents

Block 2
Investigating home

Chapter 1

Exploring home: sociology, social divisions and social change

by Karim Murji and Elizabeth Silva

Contents

Introduction

In this chapter the study of the home is approached through two of the key concerns of sociology – social change and social divisions. How does the home provide a setting through which social change is evident? In what ways does the home reflect and reproduce social divisions? To help you start thinking about this, look at Activity 1.

Activity 1

(a) Make a quick list of the places you have lived, the reasons for moving and which ones felt most like home to you.

(b) Now think about your current home, or any other home you recall. Was there a pattern to who did what kind of work in your home?

Discussion

(a) Thinking about places you have lived may have led you to consider the ways in which there are, or could be, many reasons and causes for moving home. Changing jobs, moving to other countries or other parts of the same country, or changes in family life are some examples. These suggest that moving home can be prompted by personal issues (e.g. the birth of a new child) or economic issues (e.g. changes in the job market). How these sorts of personal and individual changes can be related to a bigger sociological picture is taken up in the next section.

(b) The question of who does what kind of work in the home begins to bring out issues of inequality, particularly gender inequality, but also inequalities due to class and age. This will be explored later in the chapter by introducing ideas about uses of time and space in the home.

The changing presence and role of technology in the home can also help us to identify social change, and provide a way of understanding social divisions and inequalities. How technologies structure time and space in the home is a key concern of this chapter. These dimensions – time and space – are useful in understanding social divisions and inequalities between groups of people in the home.

The term 'social divisions' refers to entrenched, persistent and continuing differences between groups of people, which sociologists explain in terms of categories such as social class, gender, age, ethnicity/race, sexuality and disability. In these categories of social division, patterns of inequality tend to recur over time and across generations. Although some degree of social change is possible – meaning people are not necessarily trapped by their circumstances at birth – an overall picture of inequalities between groups persists over time. As the reasons for these patterns are more than a matter of individual or group decisions, they are referred to as 'social'. It is important to add that these categories do not exist in separate compartments but are connected in various and different ways; they intersect, as will be highlighted at various points throughout this chapter.

This chapter will:

- draw on the home as an example to examine social change and social divisions

- provide a range of qualitative and quantitative evidence to explore social change and social divisions

- show how sociologists draw on ideas of time and space to explore differences and inequalities in the home, particularly in relation to gender and age divisions.

Section 1, 'Home and social change', examines historical changes in household composition and the link between personal lives and social trends.

Section 2, '"All mod cons": time and inequality', focuses on the practices of doing the laundry in relation to gender and the uses of domestic time.

Section 3, 'Space at home: from codes to zones' explores intergenerational differences regarding the uses of home space.

Time and space, and gender and generation, frame this chapter's exploration of social divisions in the home.

1 Home and social change

Social change includes both large- and small-scale changes. The home is an interesting setting in which change can be observed. Living in cities or towns, relationship choices, to marry or not, to have children or not, or to live together in small or larger units are all instances that contribute to the sense of social changes when considered at a large scale or at societal level.

Thinking about the places you have lived in Activity 1 may have led you to consider how these places have changed. For example, you could have moved from a parental home to live with friends or a partner; you may have had your own family home, or lived on your own. Perhaps you thought about the people you lived with in each of the homes you had. The changes of your own home living combined with many other individuals' home lives gives a pattern of what home life is like on a larger scale.

At a national level, the composition of the home and how it has changed over time provides a way of tracing social change. To look at this, large-scale **survey** data provides a snapshot of **household** composition at various points in time. Exploring changes over time reveals the nature or direction of social change. Activity 2 will help you to see this point.

Survey
A method of collecting data on more than one case at a single point in time. It can involve a structured interview or a self-completed questionnaire. It provides a way of statistically analysing the relationship between variables.

Household
The definition of a household has changed over time. The Office for National Statistics (ONS) treats any group of people at the same address (not including communal buildings) as a household whether they are family or non-family, or whether single- or multiple-person homes.

Activity 2

(a) Look at the data in Table 1.1. You may notice that some boxes do not contain data. Why do you think this is? (Two of the columns – 1979 and 2007 – add up to 99, rather than 100. This is due to rounding down to give whole numbers in the table.)

(b) Now, can you identify which is the largest change in household type over the period from 1949 to 2013 in Table 1.1?

Table 1.1 Household composition in the UK (1949–2013) in relation to marital status and presence of children

Household type	1949 (%)	1979 (%)	2007 (%)	2013 (%)
Single person	5	23	29	29
Married/cohabiting – no child	16	27	29	28
Married/cohabiting – child <15	37	—	—	—
Married/cohabiting – child <16	—	31	22	22
Married/cohabiting – child >15	19	—	—	—
Married/cohabiting – child >16	—	7	6	7
Others	23	11	13	14

(Source: 1949 in Roberts (1991) Table A.1; 1979 in General Household Survey, 2007 in Social Trends ONS, both in Silva (2010) Table 2.1; 2013 in ONS (2013) Table 7)

Discussion

(a) Some boxes in Table 1.1 are empty because there were changes in the collection of data and measurements used. For example, in 1949 data was collected on children over and under 15 years' of age. After that point, the data was collected on children over and under 16 years of age.

(b) Table 1.1 shows that there has been more than a tripling in the percentage of single-person households between 1949 and 2013.

There is a slightly different way of exploring these changes. Table 1.2 looks at the total number of people in households in the UK over the same period.

Table 1.2   Number of people in households (1949–2013)

No. of persons in household (all ages)	1949 (%)	1971 (%)	2007 (%)	2013 (%)
2	22	31	35	35
3	26	19	16	16
4	21	18	13	14
5	13	8	5	4
6 or more	13	6	2	2

(Source: Silva (2010), p. 34. For 2013, ONS (2013), Tables 1 and 7)

Activity 3

Look at the figures in Table 1.2. In this table, none of the columns add up to 100. This is because the figures for single-person households have been removed from Table 1.2.

Can you see how to read Table 1.2 to work out the percentage of single-person households? Look only at the columns for 2007 and 2013.

Discussion

By adding up the percentages in the columns for 2007 and 2013 in Table 1.2 you see that they total 71. 'Percentage' means 'out of 100', so to find the missing amount, 100 – 71 = 29. You can double-check this by looking back to Table 1.1, where you can see that the percentage for single-person households in those years is also recorded as 29.

Tables 1.1 and 1.2 present a simplified version of data collected in government surveys. Quite often such tables aim to present or highlight the main **trends**; to show everything might produce a very complicated table. Both tables show the same trend or pattern – an overall marked decline in the number of people who make up a household. Although there has been very little change in the figures between 2008 and 2013, the overall trend is for a decline in the

Trend
The general direction or pattern of movement of something.

Blended family
A family of two parents with one or more children from either one or both parents' previous relationships. They may also have one or more children from this relationship.

Demographic
Relating to human population.

Families
For the Office of National Statistics (ONS), a family, unlike a household, is a couple linked by marriage, civil partnership or cohabitation, with or without children; or a single person with children.

Nuclear family
A family made up of parents and children only.

Macro-sociology
Examines longer-term and large-scale changes in social structures and processes of social life.

Micro-sociology
Focuses on social actors and smaller-scale

number of large households and an increase in the number of single-person households.

Although the data in these tables provides a guide about the nature and direction of social change, it does not give us any explanation for the *causes* of those changes. Sociologists stress that there are many causes that explain these changes, including changes in fertility behaviour (the decision about when to have children and how many to have), changes in expectations of relationships and marriage, and increases in divorce. Some of these may produce smaller households, but divorce and the formation of new relationships and new families could lead to an increase in larger, **blended-family** households.

Other factors to consider include a lack of housing stock, unaffordability of housing, and the state of the economy and debt levels. Increased life expectancy can also affect the change in household composition and the rise of single-person homes. The latter is sometimes discussed in rather sensationalist terms, such as a '**demographic** time bomb'. This phrase masks the fact that there are considerable differences in how long people live depending on regional location and social class.

The data in Tables 1.1 and 1.2 shows that the make-up of households and **families** has been changing over several generations. These changes are social concerns for a variety of reasons, such as the demands on housing and health services, the welfare of children, loneliness and social isolation, and the balance between the working and retired populations. This list signals how a private issue is, at the same time, also a matter for policy, politics and economics.

The image of the **nuclear family** once so familiar in TV soap operas has been drastically altered in various ways; the causes and consequences of those changes are argued about by people with different viewpoints on whether such changes are a 'good' or a 'bad' thing. Personal and career choices as well as the housing market, housing policies and the state of the economy are all bound up in the patterns that Tables 1.1 and 1.2 indicate. Therefore, personal choices are never independent of the broader economic, social and political context in which they occur. **Macro-sociology** looks at large-scale changes in society and the economy, such as industrialisation and urbanisation, and sees them as leading to the rise of the nuclear family and a decline in the size of households. However, **micro-sociology** sees the small-scale decisions that each of us makes about our families, relationships and work, such as choosing to marry later, not to stay married, to have a certain number of children or none at all, and so on, as contributing to the formation of home and its meanings in current times.

social processes and interaction.

Rather than one determining the other, 'macro' and 'micro' dimensions of social life intersect in various ways. Sociology's interest is in understanding how these processes interconnect. The US sociologist Charles Wright Mills (1916–1962) emphasised this as the distinct role of sociology – to connect biography and history: 'Neither the life of an individual nor the history of a society can be understood without understanding both' (Mills, 1971 [1959], p. 9). Mills states an important role for sociology in bridging and linking individual lives and choices with the wider social and historical environment in which they are located. While, in his view, ordinary people do not see their lives in these terms, the job of sociology is to explore and develop an understanding of those connections.

Summary

- Sociology's concerns include the investigation of social change in the home.

- Social change can be evidenced through the composition of households over time.

- Sociology connects private matters and social issues through the investigation of patterns.

2   'All mod cons': time and inequality

This section draws on some aspects of technology in the home to explore social change, and the ways they relate to social divisions of gender and age (or generation). Technology can refer to a wide range of objects in the home but the focus here is on everyday or mundane technologies, such as washing machines, TVs and computers. Household technologies such as fridges and microwave ovens are now near-universal household durables, i.e., goods that last several years and can be found in almost all homes. Nonetheless, the use of these technologies is marked by considerable disparities and divisions, such as social class.

For example, in 1956, 42 per cent of all households in the 'professional and managerial' class category owned a washing machine, but only 13 per cent of women in the 'skilled, semi-skilled and unskilled' household category owned one (Silva, 2010, p. 37). So, owning a washing machine in 1956 was a status symbol, a marker of your professional class. Today, with washing machine ownership nearly universal, ownership has become about more than possessing a functional object; owning a 'brand name' or a particular colour or design are seen as signals about lifestyle choices. Thus the type of technology, rather than the mere ownership, suggests the values and identities thought to be tied into possession of particular goods and brands. These values and identities indicate that social divisions have social, cultural and economic dimensions.

Section 2.1 examines home life in relation to a mundane domestic activity: the laundry. Investigating who washes the household's clothes raises the issue of time as a resource and a source of inequality between the genders.

2.1   Doing the washing at home

A wide variety of commonplace objects in the home, ranging from the washing machine to the microwave oven, have been promoted as labour- and time-saving devices, to make home life easier. The phrase 'all mod cons' (all modern conveniences) originated in the 1930s and was used by housebuilders and marketing agents to suggest a desirable home containing modern technology. The history of time-saving devices, though, goes back further. For over a century, homes have been targeted by manufacturers and advertisers with a variety of devices: vacuum cleaners, washing machines, dishwashers, microwave ovens and juicers are among the many objects that have been marketed in this way. Their overall purpose is to make modern life easier by reducing the amount of time and effort involved in everyday activities. This concern with speed and convenience indicates how central time is: it is something to be saved and not wasted or expended. Domestic technology, therefore, offers a good way of exploring use of time in the home.

Figure 1.1   A woman operates her new Hoover washing machine in 1956

Laundry technology in the home provides one illustration through which to examine whether time can be saved, or rather reallocated or reapportioned. Further questions to be asked are whose labour or work is 'saved' and how different uses of time as a resource contributes to social divisions. This example demonstrates how sociologists study everyday routines and, in particular, gender patterns of work and time in the home.

In the early 1900s, in the United States and Europe, electric motors were attached to washing machines to move the 'dolly' (a stick inserted into the tub to agitate the clothes) and to operate the wringer that clothes were put through to squeeze out the water. Before that, washing was largely a matter of using a hand wringer, a scrubbing brush and a cake of soap. Technological innovations progressed over the following 50 years towards automated laundering. The aim was to reduce effort, time and skill: 'the washing-day troubles are solved', 'it takes half the time to do the laundry' and 'look at Mummy's washing doing itself' were headlines in adverts for washing machines (Silva, 2010).

Activity 4

Spend a few minutes thinking about who does the laundry in your home. How much time does it take, and whose time is spent on it?

Snowballing
A process by which one research participant recruits or suggests another possible participant known to them but not to the researcher.

Participant observation
A method of data collection where the researcher takes on a role in the group or situation being observed.

Silva (2010) carried out a qualitative study of 24 families on their everyday use of technology in the home. These families were of differing social class and ethnicity, located in various towns in England; some were accessed via a market research company, others by personal contacts and **snowballing**. The researcher used interviews and **participant observation**.

In the research, the washing machine was chosen as the most useful machine in the home by all women interviewed, except two (who chose the cooker). One participant who chose the washing machine, Lindsay Wells, said: 'I couldn't cope without the washing machine – I'd go into panic stations ... without the washer.' However, when men were asked the same question, responses were quite different. Colin Addison said the TV was the most useful machine in his home and the washing machine the least useful. Yet, the Addison household, with two adults and four children (one being a baby), did 29 loads of laundry every week. Other families also had quite intensive laundry practices: three households did 20 loads a week, six households did between eight and 14 loads, 11 did between four and seven, and only in three homes were less than three loads of washing done weekly. The number of people in the household and the ages of children were significant factors in accounting for the number of washes done.

The difference in opinion between Lindsay Wells and Colin Addison sets out starkly the difference between women and men in the study: Lindsay 'couldn't cope' without the washing machine, but the mundane process of washing clothes seems to be irrelevant to Colin. 'Put clothes in the basket and they get cleaned', said Gabriel, another man in the study. Only five men were involved in the weekly wash. Generally, men used avoidance strategies such as claiming a lack of competence: 'I might put the clothes in but […] I wouldn't risk setting it up without asking Frances 'cos I'm not au fait with how to use, or what setting to put stuff on', said Robert. Daniel said he didn't 'usually do the laundry 'cos I've got some clothes mixed up … I don't do it now … She doesn't let me use it … I don't try to get to know things like that'. (It is worth remembering this is an example of small-scale **qualitative research** and these findings should not be assumed to hold true for everyone.)

Two points of interest emerge from this. First, laundry activities in the home have changed considerably because of technological improvements. Another point to consider is that as machines made cleaning less of a heavy duty, they also had the effect of changing ideas about standards of cleanliness, thus, some have argued, actually making more work for women. So as well as 'saving' time, it appears that domestic labour-saving devices can have the effect of reapportioning time. Gershuny (2000) captures the essence of this point: 'When the laundry service disappeared, and we bought a washing machine, who had to work that machine at home?' (p. 3).

Second, even when technological development appears to make life easier, it is marked by social divisions, particularly those of gender. Studies from the 1990s and 2000s (Cockburn and Ormrod, 1993; Morley, 2000) indicate that there was a common view that 'white goods' (fridges, washing machines, tumble dryers and dishwashers) were regarded as women's goods and for housework, while 'black goods' (TVs, video players and games consoles) were treated as men's goods and for entertainment.

Qualitative research
Research that aims to understand particular aspects of social life in depth, with small samples produced by a range of methodological techniques and practices. It addresses complexity, detail and context to examine patterns of social action.

2.2   Time and inequality

The practice of laundering and the domestic washing machine indicate that routine and everyday activities reveal patterns of inequality in the home. Feminist sociologists have long argued that housework remains an 'invisible' and unpaid activity, even though it is vital to maintaining and enabling the world of paid employment (Silva, 2010; Treas and Drobnič, 2010). Housework is also a highly gender-divided activity, with women doing most of it. Time-use research provides a way of looking at the gender divide, and the home is a key setting where time inequality – both its extent and changes in its nature – can be seen.

This way of discussing time may seem unfamiliar or even strange. Social scientists make an important distinction between 'natural' (or linear) and 'social' (or actual) time. The term 'time's arrow' suggests that experience of time is a linear movement from beginning to end, over the course of a lifetime. However, the social or actual experience of time is more cyclical and repetitive. Days, weeks or even years are marked by repetition and routine. The home is a space where routine and repetition are commonplace, so it provides a useful site to investigate time use.

In the examples from Silva's (2010) study, doing the laundry was not equally shared. Men and women had very different ideas about the most useful or valuable machines in the home and there was evident inequality in the time spent on laundry. It could be argued it reflected the particular arrangements of the households Silva researched; it is not possible to generalise about all households from a small-scale study. To make a wider argument about time and inequality, it is necessary to look to other sources of evidence and other forms of research that corroborate how time is divided in the home. The following two examples utilise **quantitative research** to examine time inequality and gender.

Quantitative research
Research that generates evidence that can be counted and turned into percentages or other numerical data, for example population numbers or the percentages of people who gave certain answers in a survey.

First, Sayer (2005) presents and assesses two competing arguments on time use in the United States from the 1960s to the 1990s. The first argument is that differences in time use between men and women are converging or narrowing because men are doing more unpaid work (housework) and less paid work while, conversely, women are doing more paid and less unpaid work. The other (opposing) viewpoint she considers is that women have less leisure time because they have substantially increased paid work while men have only marginally increased unpaid work. By comparing the national time-use surveys,

Sayer found that across this time period, men have indeed increased the time they spend on unpaid work. She also discovered that the nature of that unpaid work has changed, with more emphasis on activities such as childcare and cooking. However, Sayer found that a 30-minute per day 'free-time' gap between men and women still existed, underlining the persistence of time inequalities.

Second, in a study in Australia, Bittman and colleagues (2004) analysed a time-use survey to investigate time spent using four specific technologies: the microwave oven, dishwasher, tumble dryer and lawn-mower. This research found that domestic technology such as the microwave did not save women time, and time spent on food preparation was not reduced overall. When it came to the laundry, the study found that this was a highly gender-segregated activity, with women's time accounting for 88 per cent of all the time spent on it. In contrast, men's time accounted for 57 per cent of all time spent on gardening and grounds care. In terms of actual time use, none of the technologies reduced the amount of time women spent on housework; tumble dryers increased the time they spent on laundry while the microwave oven and dishwasher had no significant impact on time spent. So domestic technology may reduce labour, but it does not appear to reduce gendered time inequalities.

Taken together, these studies support the argument that women and men use time differently. Gender is significant to variations of time because women's generally subordinate economic and social positions result from persistent social divisions that constrain their use of time. Although change does occur over time, the gap between men's and women's domestic activities remains significant.

Time-use patterns are linked to 'dual-time' schemes of home and work, unpaid and paid labour. The home is marked by social divisions in both time availability and use. In this way, time inequality is both an instrument of social division and a consequence of it. The next section explores another aspect of the home in which social divisions are evident: space.

Summary

- Technology use in the home is marked by gender divisions; time-use data shows clear divisions between women and men.

- Time use in the home is an important measure of gendered social inequality.

3   Space at home: from codes to zones

Social scientists think about space in a way that is quite different from its everyday uses. French philosopher and sociologist Henri Lefebvre (1991) argues that space is not inert and neutral. Rather, it is something that is socially produced in an ongoing way and there are meanings and consequences attached to it. He suggests that space is produced as:

- representations of space – the formal plans developed by planners and mapmakers

- spatial practices – the everyday ways in which space is experienced and lived.

However, the boundary between them is fluid rather than fixed. This section explores the concepts of representations of space and spatial practices in relation to 'codes' and 'zones' in the home.

3.1   Design and social codes

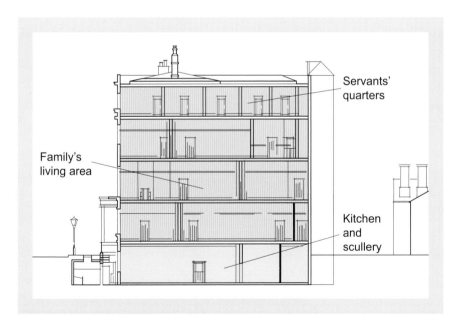

Figure 1.2   Cross-section of a Victorian house

The arrangement of space in the home reveals a social code, with the different spaces within it designated as 'appropriate' for different kinds of people. For example, Figure 1.2 depicts the layout of a Victorian house. It may look like just a house, but divisions of class and gender are encoded into its design.

Although not typical for most of the population, a large middle- or upper-class house of the mid-19th century was designed to have servants living on the top floor; they needed to be physically able and, often, young to cope with the demands of moving around the house. Segregated staircases and hallways were designed to avoid encounters between masters and servants. Some houses even had separate spaces and staircases for women and men. Smoking rooms were men's spaces; drawing and morning rooms were intended for women. These separate spaces signalled both a sexual and a social-class code of appropriate spaces for men and women, and for the lower and upper classes.

The design of home spaces is marked by cultural and historical patterns of class divisions and gender relations. Historical patterns have varied significantly within and between countries, and still do. Today, lack of space and concerns about security (heightened in countries of great inequalities) has led to wealthy owners being 'guarded' within high buildings with gates or walls by concierges, porters and security personnel. However, such properties can also be markers of luxury and wealth. Even the design of contemporary luxury apartments can reveal a version of the Victorian household model. For instance, the floor plan of an expensive apartment block (Figure 1.3) shows a service entrance and servants' quarters that are separate from the main living area of the family.

The presence of live-in servants is not common and most people have simpler living arrangements. But the examples of the Victorian house and contemporary apartments suggest how space can be viewed sociologically. The design of a home and the arrangement of space reflect the social divisions and social relations within it.

These floor layouts are examples of Lefebvre's *representations of space* – plans that contain and reflect the planners' and owners' idealised sense of social relations within that space.

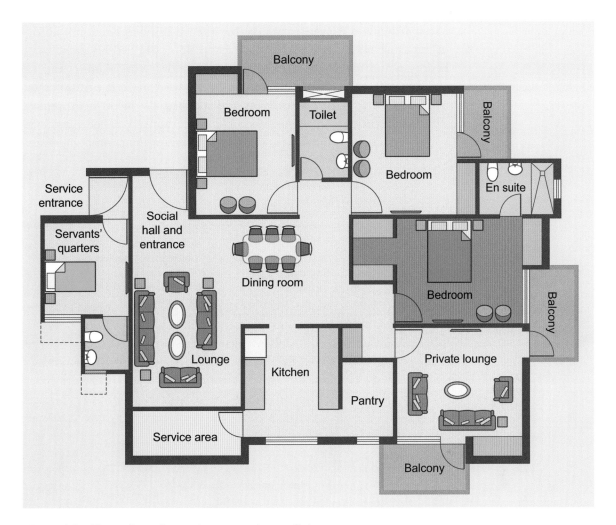

Figure 1.3   Floor plan of a contemporary luxury flat

3.2   Lived space in the home

The ways in which space is lived in within the home (spatial practices) can be seen in an example taken from Silva's (2010) study, which explores the relationship between space, objects and technology in the home.

The Churchills are a family – a man, a woman and three children – living in a semi-detached Victorian house in London. When Diane (43) and Marc (44) started living together, Diane's twin brothers lived with them. The four of them bought the house jointly in the mid-1980s. Later on, Diane and Marc bought the brothers' share. One of the twins had married and moved elsewhere but the other twin, Kirk, still lived in the same house in a bed-sit on the top floor. He had his own bedroom and bathroom. He did his own laundry, worked shifts and was rarely at home. When he was in, he ate with the rest of the family. The children enjoyed his company and watched TV in his bedroom. The family chose to have no other TV in the house but had four computers and a games console instead. They ate their meals together.

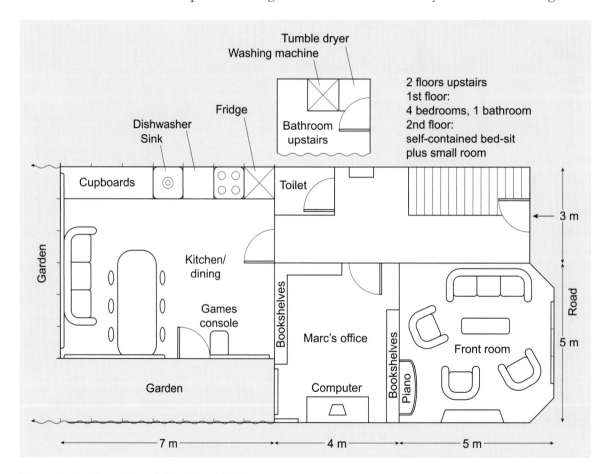

Figure 1.4   Floor plan of the Churchills' house

The ways the household worked had a lot to do with how it had evolved. Daily life was managed in an egalitarian way, so it was not assumed that Diane was responsible for housework. The children were involved in a number of housework tasks: Greg (15) cooked the evening meal twice a week and usually tidied up after meals, while Hannah (11) and Alice (9) unloaded the dishwasher and the washing machine, hung up clothes to dry, dried some in the tumble dryer, and checked and distributed clothes on people's beds once they were ready.

Their use of space in the house was also distinctive (Figure 1.4). The front room belonged to Diane and Marc. They went into it every evening after dinner to have coffee, talk and listen to music, or to read. The children only went there if invited. Marc's office occupied the second room downstairs. The kitchen/dining area had been recently refurbished. This was the place for family sociability. So, in this house there were designated spaces for particular sorts of relationships. As a family they met predominantly in the kitchen, because the couple had their own private room and Marc's work had its dedicated space.

This description of one family and their home is an example; it is useful to illustrate a point without claiming that it is typical. The size of the house, and the fact that it contains a separate bedsit flat, indicates the higher social class of the occupants. The ways in which space is divided and used suggests gender and generational relations within the house. Diane and Marc Churchill were both in professional executive occupations – Marc was at home nearly full time while Diane worked outside the home full time – and they dealt with gender roles in flexible ways. Greg and his father were in charge of cooking, while the daughters shared the laundry duties.

However, they also employed a female cleaner. The vast majority of this kind of paid domestic work is done by women on quite low levels of pay; the phrase 'cash-rich, time-poor' captures this sense of wealthy, busy professional people who draw on domestic assistants to manage their 'work–life balance'.

The role that everyday technologies play in the Churchill home is revealing of their domestic gender and generational arrangements. For all the egalitarian concerns exhibited by Diane and Marc, the distribution of tasks between the three children was somewhat gendered (the boy cooks; the girls do laundry) and divided by age.

The children could only watch a TV in their uncle's bedroom since their parents did not own one. TVs are one of the most widely used consumer durables, found in almost every home in Britain. A look at the history of this everyday object reveals how much it has changed social relations and the use of space in the home. As TV ownership spread in the 1950s, a question arose for families about which room it belonged in, as each room already had a predefined purpose. As Spigel (1992) shows, families had to literally make room for the TV in the home. Most families decided to put it in the front room, a decision that marked an incursion into a household space that had been reserved for adults, leading in some way to the creation of the 'living room' or 'lounge', as it is now often called. Open-plan spaces such as linked living and dining rooms – and kitchens – from which the TV can be viewed (Livingstone, 2007) are an extension of the central role and place of the TV as a household object, shaping the use of space in the home. There is also some evidence, albeit somewhat dated, that some 'new' gender divisions and roles were produced, such as the domination of the remote control by men, and their preference for sports over other kinds of ('women's') programmes (Morley, 2000).

Activity 5

Now that you have looked at the outline of a Victorian house and a contemporary luxury apartment, and read about the Churchills, how do these situations differ from your own residence and living arrangements?

Discussion

This activity may have helped you to think about how space in your own home reflects social relations. It may be quite different from the examples you have just read about but, in common with those examples, it is likely to be shaped by social divisions such as class, gender and age. The examples of the TV and the Churchill household are instances of spatial practices – how space is mapped onto actual use and how it is lived on an everyday basis. The idea of zones described in the following sections extends this way of thinking about spaces.

3.3   Zone 1: young people and bedroom culture

The idea of a 'bedroom culture' originated in the 1970s as a criticism of the predominant focus by sociologists on what boys and young men did in public places such as the street, schools or football grounds. 'Bedroom culture' provided a gender-based response to the emphasis on 'street culture' as a masculinised space. Feminist scholars such as McRobbie and Garber (1976) looked at what girls did. In the home they highlighted the bedroom as a space where girls and young women were active in developing their identities by putting up posters, reading magazines and practising applying make-up. The bedroom was a private space, physically apart from parents and sometimes from siblings too. It provided a means of managing social relations within the home by keeping a space, or a zone, separate from the adult world.

Figure 1.5   'Bedroom culture' saw the bedrom as a space where girls and young women actively developed their identities

It was suggested earlier in this chapter that housing design can be viewed in terms of 'codes'. Lincoln (2004) suggests 'zone' is a better term to understand something such as bedroom culture. She argues that this is because codes are cultural and symbolic, but the notion of zones stresses the physical arrangement of objects – furniture and technology – in a particular space. It is therefore more concerned with how material objects are arranged and their role in structuring space and social relations. Whereas codes tend to keep people, spaces and objects apart, Lincoln (2004) uses zones as a way of thinking about how spaces might also overlap and integrate. Among the most significant objects she identifies are the TV, music system, computer and mobile phone. The increased presence of these in some homes may lead families to spend more time together – in a living room, for instance. It may also lead to more separation within a household as people do things on their own, such as surfing the internet, for example.

Activity 6

Think about the contents of your bedroom when you were a child – the furniture and other objects, such as technology, in it. Did the arrangement of these objects reflect your own style or personality? What difference do you think that being female or male made to your experience of a 'bedroom culture'?

To think about the bedroom as a zone emphasises the presence of material objects in that space, and how those objects shape and contribute to social relations in the home. In recent decades, there has been a growth in multiple TV sets in the home as well as a proliferation of actual television channels due to the spread of satellite and cable services. However, the rise in digitally connected households is more marked than the increase in the number of TVs per household, with TV ownership in the UK showing signs of slowing since 2010 (BARB, 2015). The rapid development of digital and communication technologies is commonly regarded as heralding a generational divide. At the time of writing, young people under 16 are sometimes referred to as 'digital natives' because such resources have been present throughout their lives, whereas older people are 'digital immigrants'. However, even though mobile technology is more of an ever-present phenomenon in the lives of young people, terms such as 'natives' and 'immigrants' exaggerate the extent to which older people are resistant to technology. There is evidence that older people divide almost equally between being critical and adapting in terms of accepting technology (Wahl and Mollenkopf, 2003).

Livingstone (2007) has pointed out that in 'media-rich' homes and bedrooms, there has been a multiplication of domestic media goods as well as a diversification as more and different media goods are acquired. She stresses that these developments have tended to make bedrooms, especially for children in more prosperous households who have a room of their own, into spaces for private consumption of media, and of TV and the internet in particular. In turn, the living room becomes a shared space for when families spend time together. Her research shows that the bedroom becomes a space where young people say they can 'escape' to and have some 'freedom' from parental supervision. 'Living together separately' is a phrase that captures this sense of family life. Thinking back to bedroom culture in the 1970s, however, there are still continuities as young people then also sought the bedroom as a space to keep apart from the rest of the household. In spite of this, technological developments can also be seen as bringing people together in different ways – for example, talking to friends and relatives via social media and video-chat facilities, such as Skype. This indicates that the relationship between technology and social change does not just go in one direction.

Who uses which zones in the home is divided by social class – many young people share a bedroom – as well as gender, so all these divisions intersect rather than exist in separate compartments. The meanings and roles of technology in the home also vary by age and the next section focuses on older people.

3.4   Zone 2: older people and kitchen technology

The beginning of this chapter mentioned the increase of people living alone and part of the reason for this is the rise in life expectancy. For many older people, living at home feels more dignified and secure than living in an old people's home. Technology can have an important role to play in enabling older people to live at home, allowing them to stay in a space that is familiar rather than strange, giving them a degree of autonomy rather than dependency. This idea of home chimes with the view that it is a safe, comforting and familiar space. Evidence supports this idea that older people are the group least likely to move home. UK policy think tank the Joseph Rowntree Foundation found that only 3 per cent of households with no one aged under 55 move every year; it also found that people aged 75 years or older are least likely to move home (Pannell et al., 2012). There are probably many reasons for this, including, for example, economic factors and family ties.

The discussion of older people and technology at home is sometimes framed in terms of 'assisted living' – the use of technological aids that can enable people to adapt the home environment, thus allowing them to remain at home. This includes adaptations to the home that make mobility easier. However, in addition, the place of 'ordinary' everyday technologies is useful for thinking about the use of space in the home. Research finds that central heating, TVs and washing machines appear to have greater impact on the quality of home life than more 'cutting-edge' technologies (Wahl and Mollenkopf, 2003), with older people stressing that the design and usability of these everyday objects matter more for the quality of the home environment than owning the latest technological aids.

A research study on the kitchen and how it can be adapted for older people at home was carried out at The Open University (Maguire et al., 2013). The purpose of the study was to identify ways of assisting people to maintain their desired independence and autonomy at home. Such studies investigate how the zone of the kitchen is actually lived in and used. Maguire et. al's study was qualitative, and used a semi-structured interview of 48 people in their sixties, seventies, eighties and nineties. The first part of the interview was about their 'kitchen history' – their recollections of all the kitchens they had known in their lives; the second part focused on the kitchen in their current home.

Activity 7

Thinking about your own 'kitchen history' will be useful in framing the rest of this section. Describe the kitchens in the places you have lived. What memories do they evoke of home life? Briefly think about the kitchen at your current home: how well suited is it to your physical abilities and, if applicable, how do you cope with any problems in using it?

The people interviewed in this study recalled the kitchen of the early 20th century as usually being the cosiest room in the house and its warmth was obviously important in a period before the spread of central heating. They also saw the kitchen as a space occupied by most or all family members. It was a space in which many different activities were carried out, including mending and making, reading and listening to the radio, playing games, as well as the activities that the kitchen is more usually known for – cooking, cleaning, and sometimes eating. These recollections indicate that the kitchen once provided a space rather like what goes on in the 'living room' of the contemporary home. The spread of central heating as well as the advent of the TV are among the technologies that increased the gap between the kitchen and other rooms in the house. Nevertheless, for the people interviewed in this study, the kitchen retained its key or central role: it remains an important hub of people's homes, a multifunctional space for a range of activites, including baking, washing clothes, writing letters, having tea with a friend and feeding the pets. Older people often find it personally rewarding to continue with familiar kitchen routines and skills known throughout their lives (Maguire et al., 2013).

Figure 1.6 Elderly people often improvise solutions to overcome difficulties with kitchen technologies

However, when talking about their current kitchen, difficulties were identified across the age range of those interviewed. These were most commonly connected to being able to reach and bend (toward cupboards and appliances); sight and lighting (problems with small-sized instructions on packets and visibility of displays on cookers, for example); and dexterity (opening jars or tins, using a can opener). In practice, the people in the study had improvised a range of solutions for these difficulties, including the use of magnifying glasses, modifying cupboards and shelves (such as using carousel shelving) and even installing a talking microwave oven in one case. In relation to everyday domestic technology (the microwave oven, cooker, dishwasher and washing machine) and others (the iron, for example), it is useful to recall how all of these have been developed and sold as time- and labour-saving devices, designed to make housework easier. Yet, sometimes these same devices can be disabling and difficult to use, not because of their complexity (although recall that Robert, a middle-aged man, said that he couldn't use the washing machine as it was too complicated), but rather because their design is not always attuned to the needs of different groups of people, such as the elderly.

While this is a small-scale qualitative study carried out in England, Maguire et al. (2013) suggest that its findings could be applicable in other countries. Problems with kitchen technology are not unique to older people and apply to other groups of people too, as you may have felt when doing Activity 7. Even well-established and quite long-standing technologies such as microwave ovens and washing machines can present difficulties for people with reduced strength and dexterity, or the inability to reach and bend (Maguire et al., 2013).

The conclusions of the research indicate not only changes in the role of technology in the kitchen, but also changing uses of space in the home overall. Kitchens were recalled by the elderly as communal spaces where a range of activities occurred. However, most of the time, the kitchen remained a separate room or space. This is in stark contrast to the designs of kitchens in recent times, which have shifted towards open-plan spaces, blending the kitchen and other rooms. Yet, the role of the kitchen in the home also appears to show a significant degree of continuity, even if the design and contents of the space have changed.

Like the bedroom culture of young people, the place of the kitchen in the lives of older people suggests that there are both continuities and changes in the ways that social relations develop over time and in the meanings of home. For most of the young people studied, the home was a family or communal space shared with other people; for some of the older people, home was a space for one person living alone. Of course, neither young nor old people are any more homogenous as groups than any other groups, and age, like all social divisions, intersects with other divisions. Yet, for both young and old, home is also about developing or maintaining some autonomy. For the young, the bedroom provides independence and an adult-free space. For older people, continuing to live in their own home allows them to retain a measure of independence. In both cases, material objects such as technology are important to home life. This reinforces the idea of thinking of home spaces in terms of zones – the arrangement of objects in space reflects the meanings of spaces in the home. The design or redesign of home spaces – and how contemporary living spaces are shaped by ideas of lifestyle, taste and fashion – reveals how people see themselves or wish to be seen, and their relations with other people and with objects in the home.

Summary

- The design of homes reflects social codes about appropriate spaces and activities for different types of people.

- Generational difference is a social division that can be seen in changing and continuing social relations in the home.

- The use and placement of technology in the home for both younger and older people is important in shaping particular meanings of home.

Conclusion

This chapter has drawn on the home as a setting to examine social change and social divisions. Drawing on these themes, sociologists use ideas about time and space, and qualitative and quantitative methods, to investigate how the home is a setting that is indicative of both macro- and micro-level changes in society. However, there is no simple or one-way relationship between home and changing social, economic and cultural factors. Sociology is particularly attuned to investigating the links between social change, the personal/biographical and the social/historical. Social divisions in the home demonstrate these links.

Social change is also evident through technological updates in the home. By looking at the place and use of everyday technology in domestic space, this chapter has brought out how time and space are involved in social divisions in the home, such as the role of gender in the daily routines of men and women at home. The ideas of particular codes and zones were drawn on to explore how space is demarcated and used in the home. By investigating time and space, and gender and generation, the chapter has sought to put across three key points:

- the home is a location to observe social divisions at work

- various social divisions are interconnected – or intersect – and do not exist on one level only

- changes in ways of living at home are closely related to wider social changes.

References

Broadcasters Audience Research Board (BARB) (2015) *TV Ownership* [Online]. Available at www.barb.co.uk/resources/tv-facts/tv-ownership?_s=4 (Accessed 26 March 2015).

Bittman, M., Rice, M. and Wajcman, J. (2004) 'Appliances and their impact: the ownership of domestic technology and time spent on household work', *British Journal of Sociology*, vol. 55, no. 3, pp. 401–23.

Cockburn, C. and Ormrod, S. (1993) *Gender and Technology in the Making*, London, Sage Publications.

Gershuny, J. (2000) *Changing Times: Work and Leisure in Postindustrial Society*, Oxoford, Oxford University Press.

Lefebvre, H. (1991 [1974]) *The Production of Space* (trans. D. Nicholson-Smith), Oxford, Wiley-Backwell.

Lincoln, S. (2004) 'Teenage girls' bedroom culture: codes versus zones', in Bennett, A. and Harris, K. (eds) *Beyond Subculture: Critical Commentaries in Contemporary Youth Culture*, Basingstoke, Palgrave, pp. 94–106.

Livingstone, S. (2007) 'From family television to bedroom culture: young people's media at home', in Devereux, E. (ed.) *Media Studies: Key Issues and Debates*, London, Sage Publications, pp. 302–21.

Maguire, M., Peace, S., Nicolle, C., Marshall, R., Sims, R., Percival, J. and Lawton, C. (2014) 'Kitchen living in later life: exploring ergonomic problems, coping strategies and design solutions', *International Journal of Design*, vol. 8, no. 1, pp. 73–91.

McRobbie, A. and Garber, J. (1976) 'Girls and subcultures', in Hall, S. and Jefferson, T. (eds) *Resistance Through Rituals: Youth Cultures in Post-war Britain*, London, Hutchinson University Library.

Mills, C. (1971 [1959]) *The Sociological Imagination*, New York, Oxford University Press.

Morley, D. (2000) *Home Territories: Media, Mobility and Identity*, London, Routledge.

Office for National Statistics (ONS) (2013) *Statistical Bulletin: Families and Households, 2013* [Online], London, ONS. Available at www.ons.gov.uk/ons/dcp171778_332633.pdf (Accessed 26 March 2015).

Pannell, J., Blood, I. and Copeman, I. (2012) *Affordability, Choices, and Quality of Life in Housing with Care*, York, Joseph Rowntree Foundation.

Roberts, M. (1991) *Living in a Man-made World*, Routledge, London.

Sayer, L. (2005) 'Gender, time and inequality: trends in women's and men's paid work, unpaid work and free time', *Social Forces*, vol. 84, no. 1, pp. 285–303.

Silva, E. (2010) *Technology, Culture, Family: Influences on Home Life*, Basingstoke, Palgrave.

Spigel, L. (1992) *Make Room for TV: Television and the Family Ideal in Postwar America*, Chicago, IL, University of Chicago Press.

Treas, J. and Drobnič, S. (2010) *Dividing the Domestic: Men, Women, and Household Work in Cross-National Perspective*, Stanford, CA, Stanford University Press.

Wahl, H. and Mollenkopf, H. (2003) 'Impact of everyday technology in the home environment on older adults' quality of life', in Charness, N. and Warner Schaie, K. (eds) *Impact of Technology on Successful Aging*, New York, Springer.

Chapter 2
Investigating housing, social policy and crime

by Deborah H. Drake and Steve Garner

Contents

Introduction

Questioning is a key component of social science investigation. In the previous chapter, you saw this investigative technique applied to the idea of home, looked at from a sociological point of view. The chapter explored the module theme of inequality through questioning time use and the use of technology in the home. It argued that what happens in the home is linked with wider cultural contexts and socio-economic conditions and changes.

This chapter shifts away from the inner life of the home to investigate the broader social issue of housing through the lenses of social policy and criminology. Specifically, the chapter explores the different ways people gain access to housing and the question of whether certain kinds of housing or housing tenure (for example, whether someone buys their home, privately rents it or lives in social housing) are linked to different social outcomes, such as educational attainment, income levels or higher or lower crime rates.

Figure 2.1   Social housing in London, England

Welfare state
A system organised by the state whereby contributions derived from taxation are paid out through a variety of schemes to ensure that those in social and/or financial need are provided with resources.

In this chapter, inequality is considered alongside the concept of the **welfare state**. This concept is important because, in the United Kingdom in particular, the social science fields of social policy and criminology have traditionally sought to examine social problems alongside different welfarist policies. This chapter will demonstrate that, even though social policy and criminology are concerned with different sets of problems, they often share a common focus of concern and utilise similar strategies of inquiry (Knepper, 2007, p. 4).

This chapter will explore:

- the role of the state, private companies and charitable organisations in shaping housing policies

- the linkages between housing policies and gaining access to housing

- relationships between housing, social inequalities and different social outcomes

- criminological investigations of housing policy and crime

- the **criminalisation** of social policy and social problems.

Criminalisation
(i)The introduction of a law that makes a particular practice illegal; (ii) The outcome of such legislation on a group that engages in the now-prohibited practice; (iii) A process whereby a connection with crime or criminal justice becomes a significant characteristic of something (ideas, policies) or in the discourse about a specific group of people, for example.

Section 1, 'Social policy and housing', investigates the way social policies function in relation to housing, tracing how different policies lead to different results in the availability and accessibility of housing.

Section 2, 'Housing: does housing status matter?', questions whether or not 'place matters' with respect to a variety of social outcomes.

Section 3, 'Housing, crime and criminology', investigates the relationship between housing policy and crime patterns and the question of whether particular housing policies can make it more or less likely that certain populations or neighbourhoods are viewed as risky or prone to criminal activity.

Define

1   Social policy and housing

The term 'social policy' tends to refer to three things:

1   the regulation of welfare and social services by the **state**, and the ideas justifying that regulation

2   the implementation of the state's **regulations** on welfare and social services. In practice, this involves a variety of bodies, from private-sector companies to not-for-profit organisations, and includes informal practice within and between families and individuals

3   the study of these regulations, ideas and practices.

Social policy can be viewed as an argument for (or against) a particular solution to a particular problem. Social policies – often represented in the form of policy documents and legislation – are produced by local or national governments or other regulatory bodies to define a problem and propose a solution to it. The important point is that social policies often define both the problems and the solutions to those problems. These problems and solutions, however, could always be defined differently by different policymakers.

Social policy *studies* are concerned with examining the legislation, guidelines and activities that promote social ends or objectives – i.e. polices intended to improve social well-being or the social welfare of citizens.

Housing is one of the areas affected or influenced by different social and economic policies. The state, charitable organisations and the private sector all play a role in shaping the policies that affect people's access to acquiring housing. Moreover, various levels of government (for example, national or local) can be legally responsible for providing housing. In most countries, this responsibility entails three elements of policy work:

1   the construction, management and maintenance of a public housing stock

2   the establishment and regulation of a system of benefits enabling access to housing

3   the regulation of private housing markets.

So what actually constitutes a housing policy? One answer is that a housing policy sets out regulations to manage housing access, allocations and markets.

The state
The political organisation that rules over a given territory and its people, and in which there are shared expectations about the practices that govern social life. It includes, for example, government ministries, agencies, the education system, the police, the criminal justice system and the military.

Regulations
Law, rules or directives aimed at controlling and managing conduct, often by setting out standards to be adhered to.

Housing, like many social resources, is distributed unequally across and between societies. The pattern of that distribution is produced by processes, rules and conventions for how people can access different types of housing (for example, procedures for buying a house, for private letting, or for eligibility criteria to access social housing). These rules or regulations do not emerge from nowhere but are made and are changeable.

Local and national governments set out regulations and guidance on social or public housing, and the state also regulates many aspects of the private housing market. For example, it establishes minimum building and safety standards; parameters for the legal relationship between landlord and tenant in the rented sector; tax thresholds for the sale of housing; incentives for lending institutions, or for private companies to build new housing; planning regulations that stipulate where new developments can and cannot be built; and the provision of government subsidies for first-time buyers. All of these elements can be thought of as comprising housing policy.

The issue of 'social' housing, however, is one that tends to be more firmly associated with state-run schemes, as opposed to the private housing market. While the idea that housing should be accessed through a private housing market is in itself a form of policy (which is an economic policy), this chapter will focus more heavily on social housing policies. (Private ownership and housing mortgages will be discussed in Chapter 3.) Social housing policies, which often tend to be state-run and managed, are intended to ensure that everyone, no matter what their economic circumstances, has access to a safe place to live. The next section begins to discuss this idea of social housing in more detail and considers a brief history of some social housing policies in different countries.

1.1   Why 'social' housing? A brief history of housing policy

Social (also sometimes referred to as public) housing appeared, in part, as a progressive response to poverty and the deterioration of some neighbourhoods, which can result from the rapid change and unpredictability that sometimes occurs as cities develop and evolve. Urban areas that were, at one time, prosperous and thriving economic centres can fall into decline as industries move on and change. When this happens, high levels of poverty can become concentrated in a particular area of a city. Such areas can subsequently become places that people negatively refer to as 'slums'. One way of tackling this problem is for governments to develop social housing policies that move people out of such areas. However, this is only one reason why a social housing policy might be developed. There are a wide variety of other problems that social housing policies might aim to solve.

Providing social housing can be seen as one means by which a state may aim to manage populations and to curtail the extent to which people with limited access to housing will become a more serious financial burden, drawing on other state resources. In some countries, including Britain, before the development of social housing policies, the unemployed poor were 'managed' by the state through workhouses (or 'poorhouses'). The goal was not to reduce poverty, which was viewed at that time as a normal part of social life. Rather, the workhouse was a place that provided work and shelter for those unable to support themselves. However, such places were meant to encourage people to look for alternative forms of employment and housing because their conditions were deliberately uncomfortable and humiliating. Indeed, these early workhouses were based on similar ideas to those that shaped early prisons in Britain – that the conditions inside the workhouse (or, subsequently, the prison) should not be better than the conditions of the lowest social class in society.

The late 19th and early 20th centuries saw the development of trade unions and other working-class social movements in the United Kingdom, continental Europe and the United States. In addition to better working conditions, higher wages and paid holidays, one of the central demands of these groups was a broader set of social rewards including state-subsidised housing.

In the UK, charities took the lead in providing workers' housing. In the second half of the 19th century, foundations such as the Peabody and Guinness Trusts built housing in London. Local government followed this lead, with the London County Council, for example, building homes in suburban London from the 1880s. The UK government followed, with the Housing of the Working Classes Act (1885). This gave local authorities the power to close down housing considered unhealthy and set minimum standards for rented housing. However, local authorities were not provided with funds for construction until the Housing Act of 1919.

Figure 2.2   Wong Tei Sin estates, built in Hong Kong in the 1960s

Figure 2.3   'Slum' clearance

In many countries outside the UK, the state did not take responsibility for housing until the middle of the 20th century. In Hong Kong, for example, social housing only came into being in the 1950s (Figure 2.2). By the early 21st century around half the population lived in such housing. In the UK, much local authority housing is now run by housing associations.

The provision of clean, safe housing is therefore a subject of social policy. This provision has assumed a number of local forms including the construction of multi-occupancy buildings, slum clearance (Figure 2.3), and planned and garden cities and towns.

Chandigarh in Northern India (Figure 2.4) is an example of a planned city. It is administered by the country's central government. The space has been planned and zoned into a number of 'sectors', each for various activities, including residential housing. The structure of the entire city is the direct result of policy.

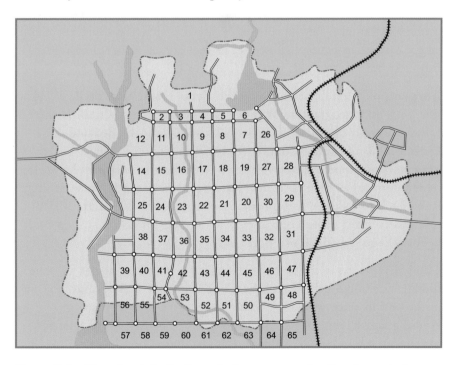

Figure 2.4   Chandigarh in Northern India, an example of a planned city

1.2   Access to housing

Access to housing is ultimately determined by what resources you have. The more money (or capital) you have, the more access: maybe to more than one home. At the other end of the scale, having minimal resources means you cannot buy a home, and therefore have to rent or attempt to access social housing. In the rented sector you often have to prove your income as well as pay a deposit worth a number of months' rent before you can rent a property. Accumulating this amount of surplus money is a major obstacle for many people, and explains why the problems of living in inadequate housing or in overcrowded conditions develop. Those groups of people who are, in effect, excluded from home-ownership and from the privately rented market are those at whom the provision of social housing is often aimed.

1.2.1   Home-ownership and social policy

Like the construction and allocation of social housing, home-ownership can also be the subject of social policy. Governments can take measures to encourage people to buy homes rather than rent them. An example of this can be found in US history.

A major policy established during the Great Depression of the 1930s was a national programme of public works and construction. If there was supply, ran the logic, there would also have to be demand. The Federal Housing Administration (FHA) was established in 1934. Its brief was to extend the opportunity to own homes to a broader section of the population than had previously been the case, by underwriting loans. Due to failures in the banking system in the 1930s, the FHA's role was to exert more control over loans, and lower the size of deposits required for house purchase.

The FHA has insured hundreds of millions of dollars' worth of state funding for home-buyers and the construction of multi-family housing in the period since 1934. It became part of the Department for Housing and Urban Development in 1965. Together, these agencies have insured upwards of 30 million home loans and, during the credit crunch of 2000–08, they replaced a sizeable part of the mortgage-lending function of private-sector institutions. The history of the FHA demonstrates that the field of social policy includes both extending private-sector home-owning and the provision of social housing.

Activity 1

Make a list of the organisations and categories of people involved in making housing policy (called 'actors' in social sciences).

Discussion

The actors you listed should include: bodies from the state, such as ministries and possibly local authorities; private-sector organisations such as construction companies and housing management firms (as well as landlords); and finally, third-sector bodies such as charities and housing associations. Each of these plays a role in providing housing and managing its allocation.

Nat'nal + local Gvt
Private Sector
Housing Assoc'ns

1.2.2   The connections between housing and other areas of social policy

The areas covered by housing policy interact with the private housing market and the benefit system. So one might ask what role housing policy plays more generally in social policy; and why housing is of interest to social scientists studying social policy.

Carter and Polevychok (2004) argue that it is important to think of housing and social policy as connected because better-quality housing improves the efficacy of a set of other social policy initiatives. They call housing 'a platform for the success of a host of other social policy areas' (p. 2) (see Figure 2.5).

For example, in relation to healthcare, which is usually an extensive and expensive area of social policy, they suggest that:

> Housing advocates must argue, with supporting evidence, that housing expenditures can reduce health care costs. Spending money on housing does not take money out of health care – it reduces the cost of health care (2004, p. ix).

Healthcare

Their main conclusion is that poorer housing quality leads to poorer health. So spending on health would be reduced by spending more on higher-quality housing. Indeed, one of the arguments put forward for social housing in the first place was to help eliminate disease. Yet

Carter and Polevychok state that housing policies are not usually coordinated with health policies. This conclusion neatly demonstrates the point of social policy studies: to identify existing patterns and relate them to policy, in order for that policy to be made more effective.

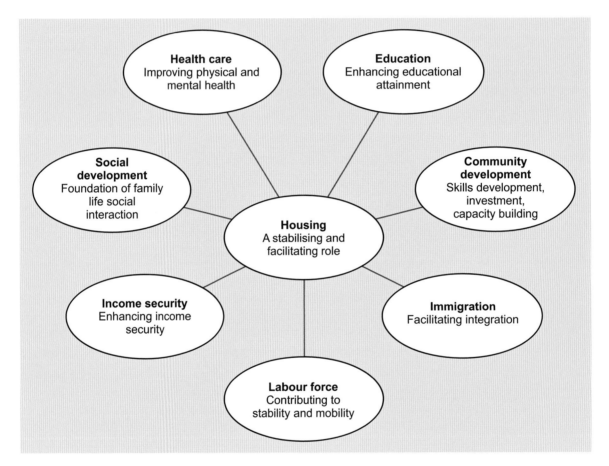

Figure 2.5   Connecting housing to other areas of social policy (Carter and Polevychok, 2004, p. 31)

Summary

- Social policy studies can investigate the issue of housing from a variety of angles (e.g. unmet housing needs, adequacy of housing, regulating the housing market, and how housing links to other areas of policy concern such as health and education).

- If one objective of social policy is to promote better social outcomes by introducing policy that reduces inequalities, the study of housing helps provide the data that would be the basis for any such policies.

2   Housing: does housing status matter?

One outcome of social policy-making is the classification of people according to their housing status. People are placed into three *main* categories of housing status, which are used in most official statistics. (These statistics are the ones collected by government agencies through various surveys – the Office for National Statistics in the UK, for example – or those of the European Commission or European Union.)

The three categories are:

- owner-occupiers (those who are either repaying back a loan on a property, or own it outright)

- private renters (renting in the private sector)

- social housing residents (renting in the social housing sector, typically at subsidised rates).

It is important to note that the proportions of these groups have changed over time due to social policy and the state of the economy, among other things. In the case of the UK, for example, the proportion of people in private rented housing before the First World War was nearly 90 per cent. After laws were passed in 1919 enabling local authorities to build social housing, this figure dropped sharply. In 2014, it stood at around 15 per cent (Beckett, 2014).

The proportions of the three groups also differ from one country to another and a wide variety of cultural, political and economic factors account for the differences in proportions.

The rest of this section will consider the relationship between what type of housing someone grows up in and outcomes in other areas of life, asking the question 'what impact does housing status have on life chances?'.

Statistically significant
Probable associations between a factor and an outcome that are not down to chance. There is likely to be a relationship, but it might not be cause and effect.

2.1   Research on housing and life chances

Is there a relationship between a person's housing status and various outcomes such as educational attainment, income level, health and wealth? As wealth typically determines one's access to housing, one would expect to find some **statistically significant** patterns.

Ruth Lupton and her team (Lupton et al., 2009) compared the housing status and social outcomes of four generations of people born between 1946 and 2000. The data was collected from people living in England, Wales and Scotland. The 2000 sample also included people living in Northern Ireland. Lupton et al. accessed data on samples of people born in 1946 (the National Survey for Health and Development), 1958 (the National Child Development Study), 1970 (the British Cohort Study) and 2000 (the Millennium Cohort Study).

The results revealed that, for the group born in 1946, social housing was usually a step up from private renting, and a stepping stone towards home-ownership. This finding, however, only remained stable for a period of about ten years. For people born in 1958, this pattern was not as strong, as more people had begun to move out of social housing and into home-ownership. For people born in 1970 and 2000, the status of social housing had deteriorated and was no longer an improvement on private rented accommodation.

Thus, data from the first cohort of the study (those from the 1946 sample) suggests that social housing provided an attractive housing option for people of all social classes. However, the data from the later cohorts revealed that the status of social housing had eroded by 1958 and had become a housing option more for disadvantaged populations, rather than households with average or above-average earnings. A key finding from Lupton et al.'s study was that 'on average, those who lived in social housing as children were worse off as adults in terms of health, well-being, education and employment than their peers' (2009, p. 1). This finding was true for the generations from 1958 and 1970, and the results also suggest a similar trajectory for the cohort from 2000.

2.2   Housing status and social outcomes

There are different **variables** that demonstrate a shift in the profile of social housing residents since the Second World War, according to the Lupton et al. (2009) study. For example:

- In 1946, only around 1 in 3 households owned their own homes. It was commonplace for people from every social class to live in social housing because of the high quality and wide availability of this form of housing. In fact, almost 1 in 6 (15 per cent) of the

Variables
In social science, a variable is a characteristic of a sample in a survey (e.g. age, gender, religious affiliation) that may have an impact on whatever outcome or pattern is being observed and measured.

country's wealthiest 20 per cent lived in social housing, along with more than 1 in 4 (27 per cent) of the poorest 20 per cent.

- By 2005, only 2 per cent (1 in 50) of the wealthiest 20 per cent, and almost half (49 per cent) of the poorest 20 per cent, lived in social housing. These changes are, in part, due to changes in the social policies that shaped the kinds of housing available.

Longitudinal study
A survey in which the sample group and/or particular variables are observed repeatedly over a period of time.

In their **longitudinal study**, Lupton et al. sought to 'control' for other differences between households in order to determine whether housing would still have an impact. 'Controlling' means that the researchers built in a calculation that took into consideration different variables, such as 'parents' education, occupation, income and interest in education, teachers' rating of child's progress, whether the child was bullied, how happy the child was, whether they wet the bed, their height and weight, and for the 1958 and 1970 cohorts, characteristics of their schools' (2009, p. 7).

When they applied these controls, Lupton et al. found that housing status had no effect on social outcomes for the 1946 cohort. In other words, growing up in social housing had no independent negative (or positive) effect for that group. However, for children in the samples born in 1958 and 1970, housing status did have a significant impact on later-life outcomes, even after controlling for other factors that might have both restricted their opportunities and forced them to rent. To put it another way, by looking at the 1946 cohort data it might be argued that a firm policy commitment to social housing might make social housing more desirable to people from all social classes. As a viable housing choice for all social class members, social housing may have the capacity to 'level the playing field' or make people's life chances and outcomes more likely to be equal. However, if social housing is, instead, implemented only as a policy for the poor and disadvantaged, it may have a negative effect on the people with no alternative but to access this form of housing.

Thus, overall, the findings show that the effects of growing up in social housing on the generation born in 1946 were neutral; but those born in 1958 and 1970 emerged worse off on all measures.

So what can be made of this survey's conclusions? The authors are careful not to stipulate that the differences in outcomes were 'caused' by childhood experiences of social housing (2009, p. 8) because it is difficult to isolate one factor out of so many and attribute a causal effect to it. While there is evidence that child development and health are affected by social housing status (Tunstall et al., 2011, for example), the relationship between housing, inequality and social outcomes needs further research to determine what matters in relation to housing policy.

This complicated answer requires thinking about the role that social housing performs. Discussing similar trends in relation to council housing (Figure 2.6), in general, Donnison and Ungerson (1982) write that the social housing sector 'changed from catering for the "neat and tidy" in the post-war generation, to providing for the "tight and needy" by the turn of the century' (Lupton et al., 2009, p. 58).

Figure 2.6   Council housing in the 1940s

Of course people's life chances are not completely determined by the sort of housing they live in. But considering the relationship between different housing policies, social outcomes and changing patterns over time in the types of housing available and who is able to access it suggests interconnections between policies and outcomes that might not be immediately obvious.

Looking for the right questions to ask, and trying to interpret the answers, are the basics of what social scientists do. There is not usually a single, simple answer. Sometimes, finding the right question is the most difficult part of the process. Often the questions are driven by the recognition of inequalities and seeking to understand what processes lead to them or worsen them. If certain social housing policies are sometimes associated with negative outcomes, how does society move to more equitable policies? It is important to realise that social science can rarely be absolute in its claims of knowledge. This is not a weakness, but a recognition of the complexities of the social world.

Summary

- Classifying people into housing categories is a technical device to implement policy or collect statistics: it is not intended to have any meaning beyond that.

- However, it is worth noting that social policy sets some of the parameters that determine how people get categorised, and these categories have real, material, measurable impacts on people's life chances.

- While research has established statistically significant relationships between housing status and other outcomes (such as health, employment and educational attainment), the degree to which the outcomes are *caused by* housing status is not clear. Housing status may be part of a more complicated pattern.

3   Housing, crime and criminology

The study of criminology and social policy illuminates the difference that social policies can make to understandings of crime. Criminology can be defined as the study of crime and also of criminal justice. Even though criminology can include the study of a wide range of topics, issues and problems that relate to crime, it often focuses on questioning and understanding the social, political and economic factors that influence the way ideas of crime and criminal justice are defined differently in different times and places.

Criminologists who want to identify the linkages between social policies and rates of crime, imprisonment or victimisation often attempt to account for the social, political or economic conditions that make certain types of crime or other forms of social harm (for example, **eco crime**, **corporate crime** or **state crime**) more or less likely to occur. Criminologist Sir Leon Radzinowicz (1906–1999) argued that identifying a single causal factor for the problem of crime was a wasted effort (Knepper, 2007, p. 5). Instead, he suggested that: 'The most that can be done is to throw light upon the combination of factors or circumstances associated with crime' (Radzinowicz, 1988, p. 95).

Criminology in the UK has, broadly speaking, considered problems of crime alongside, or in relation to, social welfarist concerns. This means that crime is considered alongside social issues such as levels of poverty, unemployment rates, the availability of safe housing or educational opportunities. However, there is no single preferred approach to investigating or theorising problems of crime among criminologists. The concept of crime is itself contested and changeable. What is viewed as a crime in one society may not be in another. Even in the same society, views about what activities are illegal can change over time.

Activity 3

Can you think of any activities that are legal in the UK today but were once illegal?

Discussion

What about male homosexuality? This was not decriminalised in England and Wales until the passing of the Sexual Offences Act in 1967.

Eco crime
Acts of environmental harm and ecological degradation; illegal and/or harmful behaviour, including threatening, damaging or destroying the natural environment. It is a term often used synonymously with 'green crime' or 'environmental crime'.

Corporate crime
Crime committed either by a corporation/business entity or by people acting on behalf of such an entity.

State crime
Crime that involves the state breaking its own criminal law or international rules, either by its actions or by failing to act.

Homosexuality was subsequently decriminalised in Scotland through the Criminal Justice (Scotland) Act in 1980 and in Northern Ireland through the Homosexual Offences (Northern Ireland) Order in 1982.

This shift can also happen in the other direction: activities that were legal can be made illegal. One example in England and Wales is the ban on smoking in public places, which came into effect on 1 July 2007.

Thus, it can be said that the concept of crime is socially, historically and geographically *constructed*. In other words, what is considered a crime in any given society depends on where you are, and on the social or cultural conventions of the society you are in. Muncie et al. (2010, p. 8) argue that: 'what we view as a crime also depends on who has the power both to define what a crime is, and to mobilise powers of enforcement against those deemed to have committed such a violation of the law.' It is evident, then, that crime is a rather slippery concept. The study of crime – criminology – is, in part, concerned with questioning and evaluating the social, political and economic factors that influence the way ideas of crime and criminal justice are defined differently in different locations. Research studies and theories of crime from one country or jurisdiction have to be tested to establish if the findings are *generalisable* to other social contexts, meaning they reveal reliable social patterns.

The rest of this chapter will focus on examining relationships between crime and housing and on the question of whether particular housing policies make it more or less likely for some people or neighbourhoods to be seen as at risk for criminal activity. Section 3.1 considers the influential work of a group of urban sociologists and criminologists from the 1920s and 1930s who formed the 'Chicago School'. Their work established what became known as 'ecological' theories of crime, which suggest that the environment in which people live and interact shows some association with crime rates. Section 3.2 then discusses the way links between housing and crime rates were investigated by UK criminologists in answer to their US counterparts. Section 3.3 moves on to consider how some social problems come to be criminalised – that is, become a criminal justice issue as opposed to a social policy issue.

3.1 The Chicago School and social disorganisation theory

Figure 2.7 Chicago slums

The city of Chicago in the late 19th and early 20th centuries was growing at a rapid rate. Social scientists working at Chicago universities during the 1920s and 1930s became interested in the way the urban development of cities (and Chicago, in particular) seemed to interact with and influence social life and human behaviour. 'Chicago School' researchers, most notably Robert E. Park and Ernest W. Burgess, were concerned with developing and testing the idea of ecological theories of human behaviour, which proposed associations between human behaviour, social structures and physical environmental factors. To test these ideas, they engaged in **empirical research** using a variety of research strategies, including social surveys, analysis of census data, and **field research** involving interviews and observations.

Empirical research
Research that is based specifically on evidence gained from experimentation or observation.

Field research
Research done outside the researcher's workplace, laboratory or library. In the social sciences this typically involves interviews or observation of some kind.

The first systematic studies of social life in Chicago indicated that the residential areas of the city seemed to be divided along lines of class, ethnicity, housing type and housing tenancy. Park and Burgess developed what is known as the 'concentric zone model' (Figure 2.8) to illustrate the way different urban environments and social structures tended to cluster in the city (Park and Burgess, 1921). According to the researchers, this model, also known as the 'Burgess model', was a representation of the 'natural' progression that takes place in cities as residential and commercial areas evolve, change and develop.

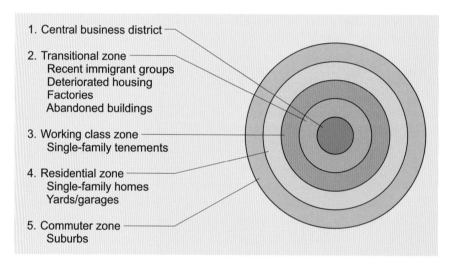

Figure 2.8   The concentric zone model developed by Park and Burgess (adapted from Burgess, 1967 [1925], p. 55, Chart II)

The core circle of the model represented the central business area of the city (Zone 1). The first inner ring outside the centre (Zone 2) was what Park and Burgess called a zone of transition. This zone was an area characterised by instability, turbulence and, in places, urban decline (Figure 2.9).

Figure 2.9   Inner-city Detroit in decline

This part of the city tended to include a mixture of both factories and poorer-quality or derelict residential housing. It was often occupied by sex workers, people with gang affiliations and drug users as well as by successive groups of impoverished migrant populations moving into the city from rural areas, the southern states or other, mostly European, countries. Different ethnic cultural groups – Irish, Polish and Italian – successively settled and then moved through this district as they worked their way out to more affluent circles, being replaced by the next wave of poor, migrant settlers. The housing in these areas was not well maintained because many property owners had purchased residential buildings on the speculation – that is, with the expectation – that properties in these areas would, eventually, become highly sought after and would increase in value. However, in the interim, the landlords would not maintain the properties or convert them into more stable homes and would, instead, rent them out as short-term tenancies (Mooney and Talbot, 2010, p. 41). Moving outwards from the transition zone was a slightly more affluent zone characterised by single-family **tenement housing** for working-class labourers (Zone 3). Suburban, middle-class housing was further out from the centre (Zone 4) and housing occupied by the rich was located in the outermost areas of the city (Zone 5), where there was space for larger properties (Figure 2.10).

Tenement housing
Buildings with multi-occupancy rental accommodation.

Figure 2.10   Suburban Detroit

Building on the work of Park and Burgess, criminologists Shaw and McKay (1931, 1942) became interested in the relationship between crime rates and different residential areas. To investigate this relationship, the researchers examined juvenile delinquency and crime rates alongside other statistical data about the social structure of populations in each zone, as measured by demographic data such as income, ethnicity and age. Conducting analyses on data from over twenty large US cities, Shaw and McKay found crime rates followed a uniform pattern and were highest in the 'transition zones' (Zone 2 in Figure 2.8), adjacent to central business districts. They also found that high crime rates remained consistent in these areas over time, despite the fact that they had a high rate of population turnover.

Activity 4

Given what you have read above, can you think of some of the reasons that a 'transition zone' in a city might have higher rates of reported crime than other areas, even when the population within the transition zone is constantly changing?

Discussion

As you will read below, there could be many reasons for this and, up to the present day, there is no one theory that can provide a single or reliable set of causal (determining) factors for the presence or absence of criminal activity among a given population. Remember the statement made by Radzinowicz that you read earlier at the start of this section:

'The most that can be done is to throw light upon the combination of factors or circumstances associated with crime.'

As is often the case with social research, the findings produced through Shaw and McKay's research needed to be interpreted and accounted for. That is, the researchers needed to try to explain why a transition zone would remain a 'high-crime' area, despite a high turnover of residents. To explain the prevalence of higher crime rates in these areas, Shaw and McKay theorised that the instability of the social environment resulted in a wide range of both conventional and deviant or criminal behaviours, which offered both legitimate and illegitimate means by which to earn a living or gain some form of social status. They argued that high levels of crime and delinquency were more likely to occur in what could be characterised as 'socially disorganised' neighbourhoods.

Social disorganisation theory, briefly defined, suggests that 'socially organised' parts of a city are characterised by a settled and stable population where people generally own their own homes and where, because of this stability, people can exercise higher levels of informal social control over one another. That is, neighbours have a vested interest in acting 'neighbourly' towards one another (for example, respecting each other's property or privacy), negotiating over disagreements and actively contributing to keeping their properties and streets well-kept and safe. Socially disorganised parts of a city, by contrast, are, according to Shaw and McKay, troubled by disorder and turbulence and are characterised by unstable, transient populations. People in these areas were generally found to be poorer and could only access housing through the private rental market under short-term tenancies. As a result of the instability of people's labour prospects and housing tenure, they were less likely to form a stable community of residents committed to keeping the peace and exercising informal social controls over one another.

The Chicago School theories on urban development and the importance of environmental influences on human behaviour have been extremely influential in both sociological and criminological studies. However, they have also been criticised and questioned by other social science researchers and theorists. Much of the Chicago

School's ecological approach was based on the assumption that the way urban development was occurring was a 'natural' process. They failed to consider, for example, whether the manner in which industrial development was being planned and implemented could have been done differently to take account of inequalities or to create (rather than curtail) opportunities for certain populations to contribute to, and participate fully in, the social and economic life of the city. In addition, the extent to which these theories applied to cities outside the United States was questionable. The usefulness of Chicago School theories in the UK is explored in the next section.

3.2   Social housing and crime in the UK

At the start of Section 3, it was stated that research studies and theories of crime developed in one country will often have to be investigated and examined to test their generalisability to other social contexts. When the work of the Chicago School is considered in relation to the UK context, some immediate contradictions become apparent.

Activity 5

Remember that key findings from Shaw and McKay's work were that socially disorganised, high-crime neighbourhoods would be located in areas adjacent to main business districts, and that they resulted, in part, from the instability of residential housing occupancies due to transient populations and a short-term, private rental market.

Now, think of an area of the town or city where you live (or a town or city that you know) that is considered a 'high-crime' area. Do you think either social disorganisation theory or the idea of a transition zone can provide a useful explanation for why that area might appear to be prone to crime? What factors would you consider if you wanted to investigate or test the applicability of Chicago School theories in a town or city in the UK, or another country outside the United States?

Discussion

This sort of test is known as empirical validity. Here are some of the first questions you might ask:

1   If the government supports social housing policies that provide stable, suitable housing for people with low incomes or limited

financial or employment opportunities, what might be the effect on crime rates in these areas?

2   If high crime rates still persist in areas where social housing is provided, does that mean housing tenancy and the stability of a residential population are not factors associated with crime?

3   If they are not, then does that disprove social disorganisation theory?

4   Are there some aspects of social disorganisation theory that still 'work', even if some parts of the theory seem to be contradicted when applied to a UK context?

5   Or is there another explanation for why crime *and* social disorganisation might persist despite the fact that social housing is provided?

Explorations of linkages between crime, housing and neighbourhoods in the UK followed different research traditions from those of the Chicago School researchers. One of the main reasons for this (as discussed in Section 1) was that government commitments to a welfare approach to social and housing policy meant that, in the UK, social housing was provided on quite a large scale, beginning in the 1880s. According to UK criminologists, the provision of social housing, and the policies by local authorities to maintain or clear deteriorated buildings, had a profound effect on the distribution of crime in the UK (Baldwin, 1979). Due to the cost of land, many social housing estates in the UK were built a long distance away from city centres. Problems of crime in UK cities were not necessarily always found in inner-city areas. Nor were they necessarily associated with neighbourhoods with a high turnover of residents. In addition, criminologists in the UK were concerned with the notion of the 'problem' housing estate.

The most comparable early study to Shaw and McKay's work that was conducted in the UK was undertaken by Baldwin and Bottoms in Sheffield in 1976.

Baldwin and Bottoms aimed to investigate how some housing estates could end up with higher numbers of people being prosecuted for criminal activity than other estates, despite having populations with comparable demographic profiles. In contrast to the work of the Chicago School, Baldwin and Bottoms found that, in the UK, a number of different factors potentially contributed to 'crime-prone'

Figure 2.11   Council housing, Sheffield

housing estates. They found there was an interactive relationship between public housing policies, allocation procedures and the reputations of particular estates. Further research conducted by Bottoms and Wiles (1986) suggested that some housing estates could maintain their criminal or respectable reputations over long periods of time, despite continual changes among residents. Thus, Bottoms and Wiles argued, the 'crime problem' of particular individual estates could not be understood without taking account of housing allocation processes. Knepper (2007, p. 57), summarising the work of Bottoms and Wiles, states:

> If an estate begins as respectable, remains sought after, and there is nothing to alter this sought-after reputation, then it is likely to enjoy a safe reputation over an extended period of time. Some estates, however, acquire a bad reputation early on, sometimes as a result of the housing department's 'dumping' of tenants regarded as problematic. Others undergo a 'tipping process' when original tenants transfer to more desirable estates elsewhere, leaving the estate to become categorised as the place for 'problem families'.

Other criminologists working in the 1970s also noted the role played by policing practices and the over- (or under-) policing of some areas, as well as whether some local authorities were exercising their political power in the way they singled out individual families as 'problematic' (see, for example, Armstrong and Wilson, 1973, or Byrne, 1974). Examinations of the policing or allocation policies that might lead to the categorisation of some people or places as 'problems' or as 'criminal' have continued to proliferate in both the criminological and social policy literature (Cohen, 1985; Schneider and Ingram, 1993; Henry, 2009). However, policy-making and governmental interventions that attempt to solve problems of crime in particular areas continue to focus on so-called 'problem individuals' or 'problem families' rather than on the range of other social and economic factors that have been shown to be associated with the occurrence of crime.

It is evident, then, that investigating the linkages between housing tenure or housing allocation and crime is a complex endeavour that is seemingly highly dependent on both local contexts and on housing markets or policies.

The idea that some people or places can sometimes develop reputations as problematic has long attracted attention from social scientists. The next section on housing, crime and criminology considers some of the ways that social problems come to be viewed and categorised as criminal justice problems.

3.3   The criminalisation of social problems

When particular areas, estates or neighbourhoods look noticeably different from others – for example, where common areas are less well maintained, there is litter strewn around or where houses and flats are in disrepair – they sometimes begin to carry a social stigma. The concept of stigma can be defined as an attribution of undesirability, discredit or social rejection (Goffman, 1963; Stafford and Scott, 1986). This idea can be applied to places, whole groups of people or individuals. Stigma attached to neighbourhoods and, by association, to the people who live in them, has real effects, such as 'postcode prejudice'. Depending on how deep or widespread the stigmatisation of a particular area is, such a label can hinder people's attempts to find employment or move into rented or social housing elsewhere. When stigma is attached to people who are categorised into particular groups (e.g. people with mental health problems, homeless people, ex-prisoners, drug users), it then becomes more likely that these groups will experience unequal access to housing because they will be viewed as belonging to an undesirable population by some of their potential neighbours or by some property owners.

At the same time, when people act in ways that other people find troublesome, threatening or dangerous, there may be calls for new policies or laws to control or prevent them from infringing on the rights of others. For example, as a response to complaints of troublesome behaviour, primarily occurring in social housing areas, antisocial behaviour orders (ASBOs) were brought into force in England, Scotland and Wales through the Crime and Disorder Act of 1998 (Knepper, 2007, p. 67). The idea of antisocial behaviour – and the subsequent policy decisions and legal frameworks that were introduced to manage it – provide a useful example of the way a social issue can lead to particular policy decisions that then slide into criminal justice processes.

Figure 2.12   ASBOs target activities that are not illegal but are viewed to be 'nuisance' problems

The social issues that ASBOs were intended to deal with were so-called 'nuisance' problems between neighbours, or antisocial behaviour on housing estates or in other public spaces (Squires, 2008). The problems

ASBOs were intended to target were generally trivial activities such as littering, public drunkenness, begging, disturbing the peace or spitting (to name only a few), which were not illegal *per se* and thus were not strictly a matter for criminal justice intervention. However, the ASBO made it possible for social problems such as these to be acted upon by authorities without the burden of proof that is required to convict someone of a criminal offence. Breach of an ASBO, however, is a criminal offence and is referred to court where the person in breach of the order is charged and tried under the conventions of the criminal law. Thus, it has been argued by Rutherford, that the ASBO 'provides a particularly striking example of the criminalisation of social policy' (Rutherford, 2000, p. 59). Significantly, the ASBO effectively made landlords and housing managers into agents responsible for implementing crime control policy. As a result, some criminologists have argued that the ASBO was, fundamentally, created as a tool to exercise greater levels of social control over the poor (Squires, 2006). At the same time, however, some of the social issues that ASBOs sought to address were very real concerns when viewed from the perspectives of the fellow tenants or neighbours living near to someone who was troublesome.

Activity 6

Taking account of the material that you have read in Section 3, how would you, as a social science researcher, investigate the question of whether or not ASBOs had the desired effect of controlling troublesome activities in social housing areas?

Discussion

Bear in mind that, when investigating any research problem, you need to decide whether your findings should be broadly generalisable or whether the question requires deep, specific and detailed exploration. This is often a trade-off but, in Activity 6, it is possible that both types of findings would partially answer the question. For example, a broad-ranging study might simply compare rates of reported nuisance activities in a range of areas and whether or not these rates changed in relation to the number of ASBOs issued in them. However, remember what has been said in this section about the importance of local context when it comes to identifying issues associated with crime in particular areas. Thus, you might want to examine one or two estates in great detail to determine whether or not people living there felt safer and/or whether those subjected to an ASBO had experienced any negative or positive effects as a result of it.

One overarching question likely to be asked by a criminologist or other social scientist exploring the efficacy of ASBOs (which would then guide their choice of methods to investigate it) would be: to what extent has the policy decision to effectively criminalise nuisance behaviours solved the social problem it was intended to solve?

Summary

- While there appear to be some associations between housing, housing allocation, general social conditions and crime, there are no straightforward or causal connections.

- For criminologists – particularly those concerned with recognising the relationship between crime, social policy decisions and criminal justice practice – established research has repeatedly demonstrated that problems of crime are the result of a complex range of social, political and economic factors.

- Investigating problems of crime requires multiple questions and methods and the repeated testing of theories in a wide range of contexts.

Conclusion

While social policy and criminology are distinct areas of study, there are many social issues that draw out the overlap between these two social science fields. Although one rationale for social policy is to help reduce inequalities, research demonstrates that this can sometimes produce the opposite effect or simply fail to reduce inequalities.

Housing is a key topic for social policy, as it demonstrates important trends in the distribution of resources. Housing has strong links to a number of other policy areas to do with life chances, including health and education. Moreover, as some of the examples in this chapter illustrate, there is an increasing range of social problems where the lines between social policy and criminal justice policy are becoming blurred. Through the example of housing, this chapter has illustrated that welfare-based policies, which might initially aim to address the needs that emerge in populations as a result of inequalities in wealth distribution and certain forms of economic development, sometimes end up transforming into policies aimed to control or even criminalise.

Thus, a key point from this chapter is that investigating the social world through the combination of social policy and criminology requires you to call into question the way different policies can impact on social conditions and, in so doing, result in different social outcomes for individuals.

References

Armstrong, D. and Wilson, M. (1973) 'City politics and deviancy amplification', in Taylor, I. and Taylor, L. (eds) *Politics and Deviance*, Harmondsworth, Penguin.

Baldwin, J. (1979) 'Ecological and areal studies in Great Britain and the United States', *Crime and Justice*, vol. 1, pp. 29–66.

Baldwin, J. and Bottoms, A.E. (1976) *The Urban Criminal*, London, Tavistock.

Beckett, D. (2014) *Trends in the United Kingdom Housing Market, 2014* [Online], London, ONS. Available at www.ons.gov.uk/ons/dcp171766_373513.pdf (Accessed 1 March 2015).

Bottoms, A.E. and Wiles, P. (1986) 'Housing tenure and residential community crime careers in Britain', *Crime and Justice*, vol. 8, pp. 101–62.

Burgess, E.W. (1967 [1925]) 'The growth of the city: an introduction to a research project', in Park, R.E, Burgess, E.W. and McKenzie, R.D. (eds) *The City*, Chicago, IL, University of Chicago Press

Byrne, D.S. (1974) *Problem Families: A Housing Lumpenproletariat,* Working Paper in Sociology, no. 5, Durham, University of Durham.

Carter, T. and Polevychok, C. (2004) *Housing is Good Social Policy*, Research Report F50, Ottawa, Canadian Policy Research Networks.

Cohen, S. (1985) *Visions of Social Control: Crime, Punishment and Classification*, Cambridge, Polity Press.

Donnison, D. and Ungerson, C. (1982) *The Future of Council Housing*, Harmondsworth, Penguin.

Goffman, E. (1963) *Stigma: Notes on the Management of Spoiled Identity*, Englewood Cliffs, NJ, Prentice Hall.

Henry, S. (2009) 'Social construction of crime', in Miller, J.M. (ed.) *21st Century Criminology: A Reference Handbook*, Thousand Oaks, CA, Sage, pp. 297–305.

Lupton, R., Tunstall, R., Sigle-Rushton, W., Obolenskaya, P., Sabates, R., Meschi, E., Kneale, D. and Salter, E. (2009) *Growing up in Social Housing in Britain: A Profile of Four Generations, 1946 to the Present Day* [Online], York, Joseph Rowntree Foundation. Available at www.jrf.org.uk/sites/files/jrf/social-housing-britain-FULL.pdf (Accessed 9 February 2014).

Knepper, P. (2007) *Criminology and Social Policy*, London, Sage.

Mooney, G. and Talbot, D. (2010) 'Global cities, segregation and transgression', in Muncie, J., Talbot, D. and Walters, R. (eds) *Crime: Local and Global*, Devon, Cullompton, Willan/Milton Keynes, The Open University , pp. 37–70.

Muncie, J., Talbot, D. and Walters, R. (2010) *Crime: Local and Global*, Devon, Cullompton, Willan/Milton Keynes, The Open University .

Park, R.E. and Burgess, E.W. (1921) *Introduction to the Science of Sociology*, Chicago, University of Chicago Press.

Radzinowicz, L. (1988) *The Cambridge Institute of Criminology: Its Background and Scope*, London, HMSO.

Rutherford, A. (2000) 'An elephant on the doorstep: criminal policy without crime in New Labour's Britain', in Green, P. and Rutherford, A. (eds) *Criminal Policy in Transition*, Oxford, Hart Publishing, pp. 33–62.

Shaw, C.R. and McKay, H.D. (1931) *Social Factors in Juvenile Delinquency,* Washington, US Government Printing Office.

Shaw, C.R. and McKay, H.D. (1942) *Juvenile Delinquency and Urban Areas*, Chicago, University of Chicago Press.

Schneider, A. and Ingram, H. (1993) 'The social construction of target populations: implications for politics and policy', *The American Political Science Review*, vol. 87, no. 2, pp. 334–47.

Squires, P. (2006) 'New Labour and the politics of antisocial behaviour', *Critical Social Policy*, vol. 26, no. 1, pp. 144–68.

Squires, P. (ed.) (2008) *ASBO Nation: The Criminalisation of Nuisance*, Bristol, Policy Press.

Stafford, M.C. and Scott, R.R. (1986) 'Stigma, deviance and social control: some conceptual issues', in Ainlay, S.C, Becker, G. and Coleman, L.M. (eds) *The Dilemma of Difference*, New York, Plenum.

Tunstall, B., Lupton, R., Kneale, D. and Jenkins, A. (2011) 'Growing up in social housing in the new millennium: housing, neighbourhoods and early outcomes for children born in 2000', *CASE Paper*, no. 143, London, CASE, LSE.

Chapter 3
Home-ownership: investment, wealth and inequality

by Alan Shipman

Contents

Introduction

Public policy towards housing has changed over time. For example, governments that were once big providers of housing as part of their social policy have encouraged the growth of non-profit housing associations and private-sector landlords as alternative sources of rented homes. Governments have also promoted home-ownership – helped by the aspiration of many households to become 'owner-occupiers', and their increasing scope for doing so as their incomes rise and the necessary mortgage loans become available. This chapter examines the causes, and some of the consequences, of rising owner-occupation, which has been happening across a number of countries in recent decades. It pays particular attention to financial aspects of home-buying and the collective results of treating housing as an **asset**.

Asset
A durable item that is expected to generate a flow of future income and/or can be sold to raise money.

This chapter will explore:

- the ways that households might gain economically from owning their homes, and evidence that this is a motive for buying them

- the theories and evidence that social scientists can use to test propositions on the causes and impacts of home-buying behaviour

- the impact of property purchases on the inequality of wealth distribution

- the wider economic impact of widespread house purchase, and of bank lending to enable this – including worsening affordability problems and financial sector instability.

Section 1, 'Renting or buying: which do people prefer?', examines evidence for people preferring ownership to renting.

Section 2, 'Motives for home-buying', looks at possible social and economic motives for wanting to own a home.

Section 3, 'Is there evidence that people buy houses as an investment?', considers the sources of evidence for people treating homes as an investment and not just a place to live.

Section 4, 'Housing and the distribution of wealth', examines the impact on wealth distribution when more middle-income households gain the opportunity to invest in housing.

Section 5, 'Problems arising from "housing as investment"', looks at the role of rising house prices, driven by the investment motive, in making home-ownership more difficult for younger households, and in making financial sectors fragile and economies unstable.

1 Renting or buying: which do people prefer?

During the 20th century, an increasing number of households became owners of the homes they lived in. Figure 3.1 shows changes in the proportion of homes that were owner-occupied, between 1985 and 2004, for various groupings of countries in the Organisation for Economic Cooperation and Development (**OECD**). The proportion of the housing stock in owner-occupation rose everywhere – although it remained much higher in eastern and southern Europe and in English-speaking countries (including the United States and United Kingdom) than in the west or north of continental Europe.

OECD
Paris-based forum of major world economies, with 34 members in 2014.

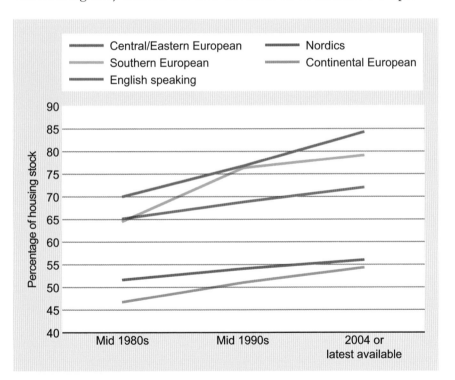

Figure 3.1 Proportion of homes that were owner-occupied, selected OECD countries, 1985–2004 (Andrews et al., 2011, Figure 6)

The division between owner-occupiers (people who own their home) and tenants (people who rent their home) varies widely across regions, as Figure 3.1 suggests. But as countries' national income (Gross Domestic Product or GDP) grows, home-ownership tends to increase. In England and Wales, 64 per cent of households owned their homes

2011 –
64% owned
England + Wales.

United Kingdom
The United Kingdom (UK) and Great Britain are sometimes used interchangeably although the accurate designation is that Great Britain refers to England, Scotland and Wales, while the UK includes Northern Ireland as well as those three nations.

in 2011, outright or with a mortgage. The remaining 36 per cent were tenants, renting from a private or social landlord. This was a substantial turnaround from a century earlier. In 1918, 77 per cent of households in England and Wales lived in rented accommodation and only 23 per cent were owner-occupiers (ONS, 2013).

The number of people who own their home may be less than the number of those who wish to do so, because many are waiting to buy when circumstances allow. Table 3.1 summarises the results of a survey conducted in the **United Kingdom** in 2011 by the polling organisation YouGov, commissioned by the Council of Mortgage Lenders (CML). A sample of 2056 adults were asked what type of tenure they have now, and what type they expected to have in two years' time and in ten years' time.

Table 3.1 Tenure preferences by current tenure (percentages)

Current tenure **now**	Preferred tenure in two years				Preferred tenure in ten years			
	Owning	Private renting	Social renting	Relatives/ friends	Owning	Private renting	Social renting	Relatives/ friends
Owning	92	1	1	1	91	1	2	0
Private renting	47	37	4	3	76	12	4	0
Social renting	36	3	48	2	43	2	44	1
Relatives/ friends	48	14	5	15	78	5	4	1
All tenures	74	7	8	3	81	3	7	0

Source: Pannell (2012) Table 5

Quantitative Evidence.

For people in this sample, selected to be representative of the population as a whole, home-ownership was preferable to any type of renting. The first row shows that, of those in the sample who were already owner-occupiers, 92 per cent expected to remain so in two years' time, and 91 per cent in ten years' time. The fourth row shows that, of those who were living with relatives (including parents) or friends at the time of the survey, 48 per cent aspired to be owner-occupiers within two years, and 78 per cent within ten years.

Activity 1

What does Table 3.1 tell you about the housing aspirations of those who were renting accommodation privately at the time of the survey? Did most of these households aspire to move into home-ownership in two years' or ten years' time?

[handwritten margin note: 47% in 2 But 76% in 10yr]

Discussion

The aspiration towards home-ownership is equally clear among private tenants in the CML survey, especially in the longer term. Forty seven per cent expected to be home-owners in two years, and 76 per cent in ten years. Only 37 per cent expected still to be renting privately in two years, and this proportion falls to 12 per cent after ten years.

[handwritten margin note: probably due to the large deposits req'd for home ownership or it may be higher]

For social-housing tenants in the survey, the expectation of moving on to ownership is less strong. Forty eight per cent still expected to be renting social housing after two years, while 44 per cent still expected to be living in social housing even after ten years. While this might mean that more than 40 per cent of social-housing tenants were happy with their present tenure type, it may also indicate that some were resigned to staying in rented accommodation because of their social and financial situation, regarding future ownership as unrealistic rather than undesirable. More than one in three (36 per cent) would prefer to be owner-occupiers in two years' time, and this proportion grows to 43 per cent for the ten-year horizon.

Unlike the ONS data quoted earlier, which comes from a census (survey) of the whole population, the CML data comes from a sample of people and so is subject to error. In statistical terms, error is the difference between the 'true' value of a variable and the value obtained from observation or sampling. The CML survey was also conducted online, which may have made it harder to keep the sample representative, since around 25 per cent of UK adults still had no fast broadband connection at the time (Ofcom, 2014). It could also be argued that the CML, an association of financial companies offering mortgage loans, had a commercial interest in demonstrating suppressed demand for home-buying – though it used an "independent" firm, YouGov, to ensure the research was independent. Despite these caveats, the survey provides evidence that most households prefer

[handwritten margin note: Question]

owner-occupation to renting. Overall, 74 per cent expected or aspired to own their own home two years after the survey (around 2014), and 81 per cent saw themselves as home-owners within ten years.

Summary

- There is evidence (at least in the UK) that most households prefer owning to renting their home. Rates of owner-occupation have risen in most higher-income countries.

- However, the proportion of owner-occupiers remains much lower in some countries; and some survey evidence may overstate the number who will actually switch from renting to owning in future.

2 Motives for home-buying

This section looks from an economic perspective at the possible social and economic motives for wanting to own a home.

2.1 A social motive? Ownership and social outcomes revisited

One powerful reason why people might want to buy their home, rather than rent it from someone else, has already been suggested in Chapter 2. Home-owners tend to be better off than renters on a number of social and economic measures, such as income, educational attainment and health; and there is evidence that these advantages are passed on to their children. The British longitudinal study by Lupton et al. (2009), which you read about in Section 2.1 of the previous chapter, identified a number of disadvantages associated with living (even briefly) in socially rented housing, compared with owner-occupied housing. These disadvantages persisted for four generations born between 1946 and 2000, though they were worse for those born before 1970. 'For each generation and every measure we used, those who had ever been in social housing in childhood fared worse as adults' (Lupton et al., 2009, p. 6).

In light of evidence such as this, tenants might be expected to seek an 'escape' into owner-occupation, to gain the advantages that seem to go with buying a house. However, while there is a strong association between owner-occupation and better social outcomes, it is difficult to establish direct causation running from owner-occupation to social advantage. As you read in Chapter 2, that is because the association might occur for other reasons, and it is very hard for researchers to 'control' for all of these. Changing their housing status may not (on its own) relieve people's disadvantage, if the root cause of this lies somewhere else.

Establishing cause-and-effect relationships in the social world is always difficult. For example, it is likely that having more income and wealth enables people to buy their homes, and also improves their social outcomes:

Higher income/wealth → Home-ownership → Better social outcomes

Lower income/wealth → Rented home → Worse social outcomes

These arrows, representing the direction of causation, suggest that it is being economically better off that enables people to become owner-occupiers, and also leads to their being socially better off. This would make owner-occupation an effect, and not a cause, of people's social advantage. So just moving families into owner-occupation, without also raising their income and wealth, might not improve their social situation.

In addition, some research suggests that people (especially children) are disadvantaged when their household moves house frequently, and that those who rent tend to move more frequently (e.g. Crowley, 2003; Newman and Harkness, 2002; Ziol-Guest and McKenna, 2014). So the causal process could be:

Home-ownership → Long stay at same address → Better social outcomes

Rented home → Frequent changes of address → Worse social outcomes

In this case, renting is not the fundamental cause of the disadvantage, which could be removed if the household could stay at one address.

Social scientists cannot eliminate (or control for) all the possible sources of difference when seeking to explain contrasting outcomes. That is why, despite finding measurable differences in later-life outcomes for owners and renters, Lupton et al. conclude 'we cannot be sure that these differences were caused by childhood experience of social housing' (2009, p. 8).

Activity 3

Why might it be hard to find a sample of households that differ only in their housing tenure type, and not in their income or wealth?

Discussion

Such a sample may be hard to find because of the strong tendency to switch from renting to owning when incomes rise. It may be difficult to find a large group of high-income families that still rent, or low-income families that are in owner-occupation. So a sample that contains households with identical income and wealth, which differ only by type of

tenure, is likely to be small, and unrepresentative of the majority. It may
be hard to draw statistically significant results from such a sample.

Although the causes are not known for certain, there is much research
suggesting that, over long periods of time, owner-occupiers enjoy
better social outcomes than renters on average (e.g. Conley, 2001;
Mulder and Smits, 1999; Pollack et al., 2004). This is often one of the
reasons why governments try to promote owner-occupation. However,
indirect causes of advantage (such as higher income), and undetected
causes of disadvantage (such as frequent movement), may mean that
just moving people from renting to owner-occupation will not improve
their situation. To achieve the benefits associated with home-
ownership, policymakers may have to promote other factors associated
with it, such as higher income, and longer stays in bigger houses on
the better side of town.

2.2   An economic motive? Capital gains

It can be cheaper to buy a house or flat than to rent an equivalent
property. That is, the monthly housing costs for an owner (mainly the
mortgage repayments, and the repair, maintenance and insurance costs
incurred by owners) are often lower than the monthly rent charged to
tenants. The lower cost of ownership may be promoted by
governments – for example, by making low-cost mortgage loans
available – if they believe that increased owner-occupation leads to
better social outcomes. So what look like individual preferences (for
buying a house rather than renting) can be encouraged by official
policies.

Investment
Expenditure intended
to generate a flow of
future income (in
excess of future costs);
for example, purchase
of an asset.

Even if the monthly cost of buying exceeds that of renting, the
prospect of eventual full ownership (when the mortgage is paid off)
may still make it an attractive option. People often see home-buying as
an **investment**, comparable to buying a pension plan or a **portfolio** of
shares. Some countries, including the UK, have experienced a growth
in 'buy-to-let' purchases, aimed explicitly at generating rent. Like other
investments, a house produces a flow of income. For owner-occupiers,
this is the money saved by not having to pay rent – a flow that
economists call the 'implicit rent'. Also, like other investments, a house

Portfolio
A diversified collection
of investments,
designed to spread
their risk.

Capital gain
Rise in resale price of
an asset, which can
sometimes be realised
as income.

Return on investment
Income generated by
an investment in a
given period, expressed
as a percentage of the
value of the
investment.

Inflation
Increase in the general
level of prices or
wages; expressed as the
percentage rise over a
given period.

Real (return)
Adjusted for inflation.

can deliver a **capital gain** if, as often happens, it can be sold in future
for more than it was bought for.

The income and capital gain, expressed as a percentage of the original
investment, give the 'rate of return' on that investment – also called
return on investment, or ROI. If the ROI over a given period is
greater than the rise in prices (**inflation**) over that period, the
investment is said to have generated a positive **real** return. Where
house price inflation has been greater than general (consumer or retail)
price inflation in a number of OECD countries it means that house
prices have risen in real terms.

However, home-ownership is often riskier than other investments that
a household might make. House prices can fall as well as rise, inflicting
capital losses. If they fall a long way, the house can end up being
worth less than the mortgage that was used to buy it, leaving
households in negative equity (unable to repay their debt from the
proceeds of selling the house). Property is also an illiquid investment –
that is, it is not easily converted into cash, especially when the
economy is not growing. Also, a house is an 'undiversified' investment:
for many home-owners, it is their dominant or only asset. Most other
investments can be 'diversified' across a wide variety of company
shares and other financial products, so that little is lost if one of the
components fails.

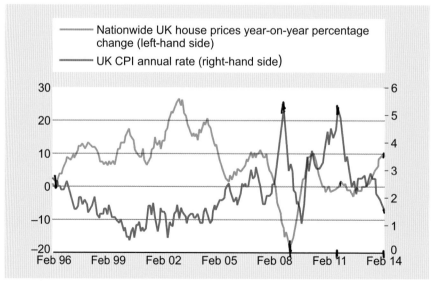

Figure 3.2 Annual percentage changes in UK house price index and
consumer price index, 1996–2014 (Moneyweek, 2012)

Despite these risks, there is a widespread belief that property (real-estate) investment will hold its value and be an effective store of wealth over time. One way to test the accuracy of this belief is to compare changes over time in house prices and in the general level of prices. This is done in Figure 3.2, which plots an **index** of UK house prices alongside the consumer price index (CPI) between 1996 and 2014. The CPI is an official statistical measure used to measure the rise in prices of a basket of goods over a period of time.

Index
A number that represents the average value of a diverse collection of items (such as a household shopping basket or a stock of houses).

Activity 4

Does Figure 3.2 confirm that house prices always rose faster than consumer prices in the UK from 1996 to 2014?

Discussion

Figure 3.2 must be read carefully because it is a graph with two different vertical scales. The blue line shows the annual percentage rises (and falls) in an index of house prices, and must be read against the left-hand scale. This index varies considerably from year to year – for example rising over 25 per cent in 2003 and falling almost 20 per cent in 2009. The red line shows annual percentage changes in the consumer price index (CPI), and must be read against the right-hand scale. This index shows less variation. The house-price index used here comes from the Nationwide, the UK's largest **building society** for most of this period, while the CPI is calculated by the Office for National Statistics (ONS).

Building society
A mutual society of savers and borrowers, usually created to assist its members to buy houses.

Comparison of the two lines shows that house prices rose much faster than consumer prices in the period 1996 to 2007. House prices then either fell or experienced growth consistently lower than consumer price growth from 2008 to 2013, before house-price inflation again moved above inflation in early 2014. Home-buyers therefore enjoyed real (inflation-adjusted) increases in the price of the average property for the first part of this period, but suffered a steep fall in real property values in the five years from 2008.

Another way to make this comparison is by adjusting house prices for inflation and plotting these 'inflation-adjusted' house prices over time. This is done in Figure 3.3, which shows the price of a typical house, as calculated by Nationwide, after it has been adjusted downwards to remove the effects of general price inflation.

The blue line shows the inflation-adjusted price of a typical house in each quarter from 1978 (first quarter) to 2014 (first quarter). This shows that there were sharp *real* increases in house prices from 1986 to 1989 and 1996 to 2004, but sharp falls between 1989 and 1992, 2008 and 2009, and 2010 and 2013. The red line has been fitted to the quarterly price line to represent the long-term trend. This shows real house prices rising at an average annual rate of around 2.7 per cent in the period from 1978 to 2014. But the trend conceals considerable quarter-on-quarter volatility, including some periods when real house prices fell very sharply.

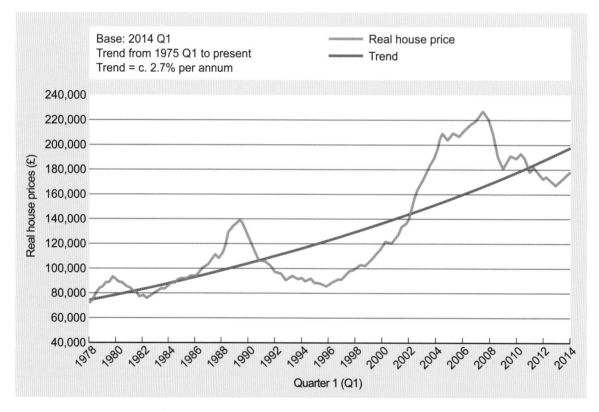

Figure 3.3   UK real (inflation-adjusted) house prices, 1978–2014 (Nationwide, 2014)

2.2.1   The importance of 'leverage' for home-buyer capital gains

Mortgage
Loan given for the purchase of land or property, secured against its value.

Usually, in contrast to businesses, people in households cannot borrow money to invest. Home-ownership is the one exception to this in many countries. If they are judged sufficiently 'creditworthy', people can take a **mortgage** loan to finance part of the purchase price of a home. Of the 66 per cent of English and Welsh households who were owner-occupiers in 2011, 34 per cent were buying their home with a mortgage, and only 32 per cent owned their property outright (ONS, 2013).

Borrowing to buy a house can multiply the capital gain if the house's price goes up. This is shown in a simplified way by Table 3.2, in which two families buy identical houses for £100,000. Both households make a down payment, representing their initial **equity** in the house, and finance the rest of the price through a mortgage loan. As the equity is the amount they actually invest, the return on equity (ROE) is the relevant return on their investment.

Equity
(1) Fairness, especially in the distribution of resources and responsibilities.
(2) The value of a house or other asset after subtracting all debts secured against it.

Table 3.2   How mortgage borrowing can multiply capital gains

	FAMILY A	FAMILY B
Purchase price (£)	100,000	100,000
Down payment (Equity) (£)	80,000	20,000
Loan (debt) (£)	20,000	80,000
Sale price (£)	120,000	120,000
Capital gain (£)	20,000	20,000
Return on equity (ROE) (%)	(20,000/80,000) x 100% = 25%	(20,000/20,000) x 100% = 100%

In this example, Family A has managed to save £80,000 towards its house purchase, and borrows only the last £20,000. Family B manages to put down £20,000 as its down payment, borrowing the other £80,000. For each there is a debt-to-equity ratio – that is, the amount borrowed divided by the equity. For Family A, it is £20,000/£80,000 = 1:4 or 25 per cent. For Family B it is £80,000/£20,000 = 4:1 or 400 per cent. The debt-to-equity ratio is also termed **leverage**: so Family A approaches its house-buying with relatively low leverage, whereas for Family B this is a highly leveraged purchase.

Leverage
Multiplication of the rise in an asset's value through use of debt.

Both families later sell the houses for £120,000, making a capital gain of £20,000. For Family A, which borrowed a relatively small amount, the capital gain is just one-quarter of the equity it put in – the return on equity (ROE) is 25 per cent. For Family B, which borrowed more heavily, the capital gain of £20,000 is equivalent to the equity, giving a ROE of 100 per cent. When house prices rise, the proportional capital gains are much bigger for those who bought with less equity and more debt.

Activity 5

Looking at the example in Table 3.2, what would happen to the return on equity, for Families A and B, if the house price fell to £95,000 when they came to sell? Would the family that borrowed more still be the one that gained more?

Discussion

If house prices fell, the relative fortunes of the two families in this example would be very different. A resale price of £95,000 means that each has suffered a capital loss of £5,000. For Family B, which borrowed heavily, the return on equity is −£5,000/£20,000 = −25 per cent. For Family A, which borrowed a much smaller amount, the ROE is −£5,000/£80,000 = −6.25 per cent. So Family B, which has the bigger positive ROE when house prices rise, also suffers the bigger negative ROE when house prices fall. While leverage multiplies the proportional capital gains in a rising property market, it also multiplies the proportional capital loss in a falling market.

Summary

- Households' inclination to buy their homes, when they can, may result (in part) from their perceiving property as an 'investment' that will preserve and expand their wealth.

- Borrowing for an investment purchase (such as a house) multiplies the capital gain if its price rises (but also multiplies capital losses if its price falls).

- Households' life chances may also improve if they live in owner-occupied rather than rented accommodation, but the cause and effect are hard to demonstrate.

3   Is there evidence that people buy houses as an investment?

Section 2.2 suggested two reasons why households might treat house purchase as an investment. The rising house price might help to protect their wealth against inflation, and it might help to multiply their wealth by generating high ROI through the use of a loan. But is this investment actually an important motive for house-buying?

One way to answer this would be to ask a group of owner-occupiers why they bought their homes. In Great Britain, the ONS did this in its first Wealth and Assets Survey (WAS), conducted between 2006 and 2008. This survey involved a representative sample of households – chosen to match the general population on such characteristics as income, age and housing status. As a survey of households, the WAS excluded people who were not part of one (such as those living in prisons, homeless hostels, student halls of residence or long-term care homes). It also did not count, as personal wealth, any small businesses owned and run by household members, or any state pension entitlements.

The WAS found that personal net wealth – assets minus **liabilities** – totalled about £9 trillion (£9 thousand billion or £9,000,000,000,000) in Great Britain in the period 2006–08. Table 3.3 shows a breakdown of this wealth into four types: property, accumulated private pension contributions, financial assets such as shares, and physical wealth (items that hold their value and can be resold, such as artwork and collectable cars).

Liabilities
Sums that must be paid to others at a future date (principally debts).

Table 3.3   Wealth in Great Britain 2006–08

Type of wealth	Net amount (£bn)	Percentage of total	
Property	3,500	39	
Private pensions	3,500	39	
Financial	1,000	11	– shares + money cash!
Physical	1,000	11	~ valuables
Total	9,000	100	

Source: Daffin (2009) pp. xx–xxi

Activity 6

The first WAS revealed that Great Britain's household wealth totalled £9 trillion in the period 2006–08, and that it had 25 million households. It found that median household wealth was £204,000.

(a) What was Great Britain's mean household wealth in the period 2006–08?

(b) What does this tell you about the way household wealth was distributed at this time?

Discussion

(a) **Mean** household wealth in the period 2006–08, found by dividing total wealth by the number of households, was £9,000,000,000,000 / 25,000,000 = £360,000.

(b) This figure is much higher than the **median** household wealth of £204,000, which is the wealth of the middle household in the distribution (the one that's wealthier than half the population and less wealthy than the other half). When the mean exceeds the median, it shows that household wealth is unequally distributed.

Mean
Average value, calculated by dividing the population into the total amount the population possesses.

Median
The value that lies in the middle of a distribution.

The better-off households have much greater net wealth, while it is zero or negative for the least well-off. This concentration of wealth at the higher end was confirmed by other WAS findings. The 50 per cent of households above the median owned 91 per cent of total wealth (or £8.2 billion of that £9 billion total), while the 50 per cent below the median owned just 9 per cent of the Great Britain total (£0.8 billion) (Daffin, 2009, p. xxi).

Table 3.3 shows that, in the period 2006–08, households in total had as much wealth tied up in property as in pension savings. As before, the unequal distribution of wealth means this aggregate figure hides some very big differences between the situations of different households. As respondents to the WAS were asked if they owned their homes, it is possible to divide the results into owners and renters (remembering that people without homes were excluded from the survey). Among the 68 per cent who were home-owners, the median household had net property wealth (i.e. their house price minus any mortgage debt) of £150,000. The other 32 per cent, who were renting their homes, had no property assets. Most would also have had no mortgage liabilities, so their net property wealth would be zero. But within the 68 per cent of home-owners, there were some whose net property wealth was less than zero in 2008 because their homes were worth less than the debts secured against them. This 'negative equity' was in many cases linked to the housing-market downturn that began in the UK in 2007.

Although housing forms a large part of the assets that British households accumulate over their lifetime, this does not necessarily mean that they buy property as part of an investment strategy. But the WAS also asked two direct questions, reported in Table 3.4, the answers to which suggest investment to be an important motivation.

Table 3.4   Pensions versus housing in retirement planning

	Strongly agree	Tend to agree	Neither agree nor disagree	Tend to disagree	Strongly disagree	Don't Know
Investing in property is the best way to save for retirement	20	37	22	13	4	4
Having a pension is the best way to save for retirement	15	35	20	18	8	4

Source: Daffin (2009) Table 8.20

Activity 7

(a) In Table 3.4, what percentage of respondents strongly agreed, or tended to agree, with the proposition that property investment is the best way to save for retirement? What percentage strongly disagreed, or tended to disagree, with this proposition?

57%   17%

(b) Can it be inferred from Table 3.4 that house-buying is more popular than pension saving as a way to prepare for retirement?

57% against   50%

Discussion

According to Table 3.4, 57 per cent of respondents showed some measure of agreement with the proposition that house purchase is the best form of retirement saving, and only 17 per cent showed a degree of disagreement. 50 per cent showed some agreement to pensions being the best form of retirement saving, while 24 per cent disagreed with this. The results are not entirely clear, as it looks as if some respondents agreed with both propositions, which is inconsistent with one option being the 'best'. Note, too, that the first proposition defines 'investing' as a 'way to save'. This might have confused respondents because 'saving' is usually thought of as putting money aside in a safe place (such as a savings account), whereas 'investment' implies taking more risk to get a higher return. Despite these problems, Table 3.4 does indicate that a significant proportion of British home-buyers in 2006–08 were motivated by investment, especially aimed at financing their retirement.

Another way of assessing whether investment planning motivates home-ownership is by looking at how the ownership pattern varies with different age groups. For two countries (Germany and the United States), Figure 3.4 shows the percentage of different age groups that owned their homes in the mid-1990s and in 2007.

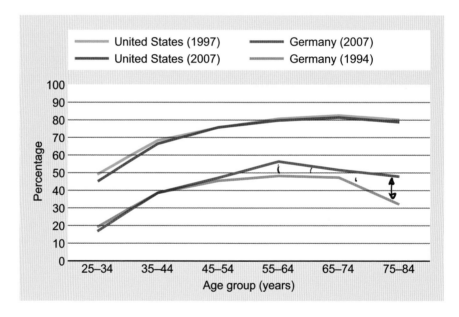

Figure 3.4   Home-ownership rates by age group: Germany and the United States (Andrews and Caldera Sánchez, 2011, Figure 1)

Activity 8

Does Figure 3.4 provide any evidence that some German households treat home-ownership as a form of investment for retirement? Does it prove that some German households are doing this?

Discussion

The data for Germany shows that, in 1994, home-ownership was lower in the 75–84 age group than for those aged 45–74. In 2007, the home-ownership rate peaked in the 55–64 age group, and was lower for those in older age groups. This might provide evidence that some households deliberately bought houses and paid off their mortgages while working, and then sold their houses (moving back to rent) when they retired. But there could be other reasons for the difference, so this would not be conclusive evidence on its own.

the gap!

Summary

- Evidence on people's motives for an action can be gathered directly by asking them why they took it, or indirectly by observing the outcomes and inferring what they were trying to achieve.

- Survey evidence suggests that, in Great Britain in the early 2000s, investment (for retirement) was an important motive for home-buying.

- Evidence that home-ownership rates are higher for older working-age households than for younger or retired households, found (for example) in Germany, is consistent with households investing in property to fund retirement; but it does not prove that this is their motive.

4   Housing and the distribution of wealth

When house prices are rising compared with other prices, home-owners can enjoy capital gains that make them wealthier. The potential wealth gains from home-ownership were explained in Section 2.2.1 using a simplified example. But what evidence is there that the increase in home-ownership has made the distribution of wealth more equal or unequal? Table 3.5 summarises the distribution of wealth in Great Britain and gives some indication of how this changed during the period 2000–05.

Table 3.5   Wealth distribution, Great Britain, 2000 and 2005

Year	Percentile	Housing wealth	Financial wealth	Total wealth*
2005	10th percentile	0	−7,637	−2,073
	25th percentile	0	−328	0
	Median (50th)	60,070	1,091	65,808
	75th percentile	172,565	16,383	197,147
	90th percentile	294,889	58,849	369,866
	Mean	115,139	21,617	137,001
2000	10th percentile	0	−5,408	−1,720
	25th percentile	0	−335	0
	Median (50th)	12,283	737	18,793
	75th percentile	81,730	11,055	97,699
	90th percentile	172,063	41,762	220,978
	Mean	60,255	14,980	75,286

Amounts are in end-2007 pounds

* also includes non-financial assets other than housing

Source: Crossley and O'Dea (2010), Table 3.1, from British Household Panel Survey

'Housing wealth' is what owners could obtain from selling their property, minus any loans secured against it – or their equity in the property, as defined in Section 2.2.1. 'Financial wealth' is the balance between financial assets (e.g. shares and bonds) and financial liabilities or debts (except those, such as home mortgages, that were included in the calculation of housing wealth).

Percentile
Segment of a population ranked by the value of one of its attributes, such as wealth or height.

Table 3.5 shows how wealth was distributed in the years 2000 and 2005. It does so by dividing the sample population (representative of Great Britain as a whole) into **percentiles**, each representing one per cent of the population. For example, if someone is in the 90th percentile, ten per cent of the population are above them in the distribution (with more wealth) and 90 per cent are below them (with less). In 2005, total wealth of £369,866 would have put someone in the 90th percentile. Someone in the 25th percentile is wealthier than the lowest 25 per cent, but less wealthy than the top 75 per cent. Someone in the 50th percentile has more wealth than half the population and less wealth than the other half. As it is right in the middle of the distribution, the 50th percentile is more usually called the median.

Activity 9

(a) Is there evidence in Table 3.5 that housing wealth is more equally distributed than financial wealth?

(b) Is there evidence that the rise in house prices between 2000 and 2005 made wealth distribution more equal? What is the difference?

Discussion

(a) One way to assess the inequality of wealth distribution is to look at the gap between upper and lower percentiles, such as the 90th and 10th or the 75th and 25th. Table 3.5 shows that, in both years, housing wealth was more unequally spread than financial wealth, mainly because the wealthiest people owned much more in housing than in financial assets. However, the least well-off 25 per cent of the population (in both years) had negative financial wealth, with more debts than assets. This was worse than their housing wealth situation, which is merely zero, because they didn't own any property or have any mortgages secured against it.

Both types of wealth (and therefore total wealth) were very unequally distributed, with a concentration of large fortunes at the higher end (above the 90th percentile), and large debts with no assets at the lower end (below the 10th percentile). This can be seen from the mean, which is the total amount of wealth divided by the total population. When (as here) the mean is a long away above the median, it indicates that a small number of people in the upper percentiles have very large amounts of wealth.

This concentration of wealth at the top is consistent with the findings from the Wealth and Assets Survey (WAS) reported in Table 3.3. The British Household Panel Survey (the source of data in Table 3.5) shows lower mean and median wealth than the WAS, mainly because it refers to earlier years and defines wealth more narrowly.

(b) Between 2000 and 2005, a period when house prices rose, people with housing wealth enjoyed a large increase. People with financial wealth also saw it rise substantially in real terms, but the proportional increase was not as great. This is consistent with the capital gains from leveraged house purchase that were suggested by the simplified example of Families A and B in Section 2.2.1. However, during this time, the situation for people with no housing wealth (in the lowest 25 percentiles) got even worse. They did not acquire any property and moved further into overall debt.

This supports a widely held finding from studies of wealth in OECD countries: that home-ownership has benefited middle-income households, who can afford it (with the help of mortgages), but thereby widened their differential over lower-income households, who cannot. 'The growth of a true "patrimonial (or propertied) middle class" was the principal structural transformation of the distribution of wealth in the developed countries in the twentieth century' (Piketty, 2014, p. 260).

Summary

- Both housing and financial wealth are very unequally distributed.

- House purchase has contributed to narrowing the wealth gap between 'middle-income' and 'high-income' households.

- House-price rises may have widened the wealth gap between households with property and those without.

5   Problems arising from 'housing as investment'

After rising for most of the 20th century, the proportion of home-owners declined in some OECD countries early in the 21st. In England and Wales, it reached a peak of 69 per cent in 2001 (ONS, 2013). One inference from this is that some people who previously owned their homes were forced to return to renting. But this is not actually shown by the data. The ONS explained its findings as follows:

> Over the decade to 2011, the number of owner occupied households in England and Wales remained more or less unchanged at about 15 million, while the number of households increased. This means that the overall proportion of owner occupier households fell by 5 percentage points to stand at 64 per cent. The number of households who were renting went up 1.6 million to 8.3 million.
>
> (ONS, 2013)

In practice, there was little change in the absolute number of home-owners in the period 2002–11. Instead, the number of households increased: partly because the population rose (due to migration and natural increase), and notably through more people (young and old) living on their own. Most of these new households moved into rented accommodation, reducing the proportion of households who were owner-occupiers.

5.1   Social problems: 'Generation Rent'

By the early 2000s, the sustained rise in house prices was making it increasingly difficult for new, young households to buy their own home. Although UK house prices dropped substantially in the period 2007–08 (as shown in Figures 3.2 and 3.3), they subsequently rose again. Mortgages for first-time buyers became more difficult to obtain, partly because applicants were typically asked for larger down payments (deposits) even though their incomes were not increasing in real terms. This led to the concern that younger people (even with their own children) were finding it harder to climb onto the housing ladder and would become part of a new 'Generation Rent' who would miss out on the social and economic advantages their parents had gained from home-ownership.

Several years after the crisis, evidence still suggested that lack of affordable housing was forcing new households to continue renting at a stage in life when their parents' generation had expected to buy. The 2011 census found that, of adults aged 20–34, 24 per cent in England and 28 per cent in Wales were still living with their parents. Most cited lack of affordable housing as the main reason, despite 75 per cent of them being in paid work (Shelter, 2014). Jessop and Humphrey (2014) found that, in 2011, 35 per cent of 20–45-year-olds saw themselves as having no real prospect of buying a home in the next five years, mostly because of unaffordability. By 2014 that figure had risen to 36 per cent.

The average tenant in England in 2012–13 spent 40 per cent of their income on rent. In comparison, the average home-owner spent 20 per cent of their income on their mortgage. This inequality prevented many tenants from saving up the deposit they needed before buying a house. As a consequence, the proportion of adults under 35 in England with a mortgage declined from 21 per cent in 2008–09 to 18 per cent in 2012–13, while the proportion of 25–34-year-olds renting privately rose from 31 per cent in 2008–09 to 45 per cent in 2012–13 (DCLG, 2014).

Throughout the period of sustained house-price rises from 1997 to 2007, government policies aimed to make housing more affordable by relaxing planning constraints on house-builders to encourage new supply, and promoting ownership by helping buyers make down payments and raise loans. But, at the same time, governments had a strong interest in continued house-price increases, which made housing less affordable for buying and renting. Because a majority of adults were owner-occupiers, rising house prices were important for promoting expenditure and economic growth (Watson, 2010), and for maintaining electoral popularity. Owner-occupiers' interest in capital appreciation clashed with new households' interest in affordable rents and starter properties, making it difficult for public policy to satisfy the needs of both groups.

5.2   Economic problems: the 2008 crisis

The sharp 'correction' in house prices across Europe and the United States, evident by 2008, was part of a global financial crisis that pushed many economies into deep recession followed by several years of slow growth and falling real incomes.

5.2.1   What caused the 'credit crunch'?

The treatment of homes as an investment in the years leading up to the crisis, by households and the banks that lent to them, featured in many explanations of what happened (e.g. Turner, 2009; Islam, 2013). Encouraged by the prospect of capital gains (as illustrated in Section 2.2), many people who had previously rented their homes decided to buy them, often taking large mortgage loans to make up for the fact that they could only afford a small deposit. These were risky loans because they made up a high percentage of the buying price (leaving little equity), and were often made to **subprime** households). Lenders offered them, in part, because they expected a growing economy to raise borrowers' incomes and expand their equity as house prices rose.

Subprime
Borrowers who are judged likely to have difficulty repaying on time; and loans taken by them.

With the number of buyers growing faster than the number of sellers, house prices rose much faster than most other prices (as illustrated, for the UK, in Figure 3.3). Policymakers encouraged this growth in mortgage borrowing by holding interest rates (the cost of borrowing) very low. By 2007, policymakers were aware they might be allowing a house-price 'bubble' to develop. Rapid growth of mortgage borrowing was causing rapid growth of house prices, which then encouraged more people to take out mortgage loans. But governments and central banks, which set interest rates, were afraid to raise them, in case this arrested the growth of mortgage lending and made house prices drop.

Despite this caution, mortgage lending suddenly stopped growing in 2008, and house prices dropped sharply. Homes had become so expensive that an increasing number of households could not afford to buy them, even if they could still take big loans. Banks were less willing to make new mortgage loans, realising that borrowers would have difficulty paying them back.

The consequent 'credit crunch' – a sudden stoppage of lending, for business investment as well as house investment – caused a severe drop in national income (GDP) and the income of many households in the US and much of Europe. Job losses and pay cuts left many owner-occupiers struggling to keep up payments on their mortgages. Their reduction in spending worsened the fall in GDP.

Summary

- Individual households' decision to use housing as an investment can have unintended consequences for the society around them. One effect may be to make housing much more expensive for the next generation of house-buyers.

- Borrowing for home investment, while making some households wealthier, has been linked to the 2008 financial crisis and the serious economic downturn that followed.

Conclusion

In light of evidence that countries experience a shift from renting to home-ownership as they grow richer, this chapter has reviewed some of the causes and consequences of increased owner-occupation. It first revisited the question of whether home-ownership (rather than renting) can be shown to improve people's life experiences, highlighting the difficulty of disentangling housing from other sources of social advantage (and disadvantage). It then focused on how homes can serve as an investment, whether this is a significant motive for buying them, and the wider social impacts of people using housing to boost their wealth.

Widespread purchasing of houses using mortgage loans was shown to have had measurable impacts on wealth inequality, reducing it in some parts of the distribution in some periods, but increasing it in others. Borrowing and buying decisions that may have made sense for individual households (and their lenders) may have adverse consequences on a larger scale, and at a later time.

The economic disruption caused by fluctuations in home lending, and the intergenerational inequality that may result from rising house prices, reveal how homes as investment assets can become a source of policy-making tension. Governments want housing to be affordable so that people do not become homeless or dependent on state benefits to pay for accommodation. But when a majority of people are home-owners, governments also benefit if house prices keep rising – enabling people to borrow and spend more, so boosting production and employment.

References

Andrews, D. and Caldera Sánchez, A. (2011) 'The evolution of homeownership rates in selected OECD countries: demographic and public policy influences', *OECD Journal: Economic Studies*, vol. 2011/1 [Online]. Available at www.oecd.org/eco/growth/evolution%20of%20homeownership%20rates.pdf (Accessed 10 April 2014).

Andrews, D., Caldera Sánchez, A. and Johansson, A. (2011) *Housing Markets and Structural Policies in OECD Countries*, Economics Department Working Paper no. 836, 25 January, Paris, OECD [Online]. Available at http://search.oecd.org/officialdocuments/displaydocumentpdf/?cote=ECO/WKP(2011)5&docLanguage=En (Accessed 10 April 2014).

Conley, D. (2001) 'A room with a view or a room of one's own? Housing and social stratification', *Sociological Forum*, vol. 1, no. 2, pp. 263–80.

Crossley, T. and O'Dea, C. (2010) *The Wealth and Saving of UK Families on the Eve of the Crisis*, London, Institute for Fiscal Studies.

Crowley, S. (2003) 'The affordable housing crisis: residential mobility of poor families and school mobility of poor children', *Journal of Negro Education*, vol. 72, no. 1, pp. 22–38.

Daffin, C. (2009) *Wealth in Great Britain: Main Results from the Wealth and Assets Survey 2006/08*, London, ONS [Online]. Available at www.ons.gov.uk/ons/rel/was/wealth-in-great-britain/main-results-from-the-wealth-and-assets-survey-2006-2008/index.html (Accessed 1 December 2014).

Department for Communities and Local Government (DCLG) (2014) *English Housing Survey 2012 to 2013: Household Report*, London, DCLG [Online]. Available at www.gov.uk/government/statistics/english-housing-survey-2012-to-2013-household-report (Accessed 28 July 2014).

Islam, F. (2013) *The Default Line*, London, Head of Zeus.

Jessop, C. and Humphrey, A. (2014) *The Reality of Generation Rent: Perceptions of the First-time Buyer Market*, London, NatCen [Online]. Available at www.natcen.ac.uk/our-research/research/the-reality-of-generation-rent/ (Accessed 28 July 2014).

Lupton, R., Tunstall, R., Sigle-Rushton, W., Obolenskaya, P., Sabates, R., Meschi, E., Kneale, D. and Salter, E. (2009) *Growing up in Social Housing in Britain*, York, Joseph Rowntree Foundation.

Moneyweek (2012) 'Annual percentage changes in UK house price index and consumer price index, 1996–2014' [Online]. Available at http://moneyweek.com/wp-content/uploads/2012/12/CPI.png (Accessed 10 April 2014).

Mulder, C. and Smits, J. (1999) 'First-time home ownership of couples', *European Sociological Review*, vol. 15, no. 3, pp. 323–37.

Nationwide (2014) *UK House Prices Adjusted for Inflation* [Online]. Available at www.nationwide.co.uk/about/house-price-index/download-data#xtab:uk-series (Accessed 10 April 2014).

Newman S. and Harkness J. (2002) 'The long-term effects of public housing on self-sufficiency', *Journal of Policy Analysis and Management*, vol. 21, no. 1, pp. 21–43.

Ofcom (2014) *Facts & Figures* [Online]. Available at http://media.ofcom.org.uk/facts/ (Accessed 10 June 2014).

Office for National Statistics (ONS) (2013) *A Century of Home Ownership and Renting in England and Wales*, Press Release, 19 April [Online]. Available at www.ons.gov.uk/ons/rel/census/2011-census-analysis/a-century-of-home-ownership-and-renting-in-england-and-wales/short-story-on-housing.html (Accessed 10 April 2014).

Pannell, R. (2012) *Maturing Attitudes to Home-ownership*, CML Housing Finance, Issue 2, CML, London.

Piketty, T. (2014) *Capital in the 21st Century*, Cambridge, MA, Harvard University Press.

Pollack C., van dem Knesebeck, O. and Siegrist, J. (2004) 'Housing and health in Germany', *Journal of Epidemiology and Community Health*, vol. 58, no. 3, pp. 216–22.

Shelter (2014) *The Clipped Wing Generation: Analysis of Adults Living at Home With Their Parents* [Online]. Available at https://england.shelter.org.uk/__data/assets/pdf_file/0007/906820/2014_07_The_Clipped_Wing_Generation_FINAL.pdf (Accessed 28 July 2014).

Turner, A. (2009) *The Turner Review: A Regulatory Response to the Global Banking Crisis*, London, Financial Services Authority [Online]. Available at www.fsa.gov.uk/pubs/other/turner_review.pdf (Accessed 10 April 2014).

Watson, M. (2010) 'House price Keynesianism and the contradictions of the modern investor subject', *Housing Studies*, vol. 25, no. 3, pp. 413–26.

Ziol-Guest, K. and McKenna, C. (2014) 'Early childhood housing instability and school readiness', *Child Development*, vol. 5, no. 1, pp. 103–13.

Chapter 4
Mapping home

by Melissa Butcher and Andy Morris

Contents

Introduction

From your reading so far you will have seen that 'home' can be thought of in different ways. It can be a space in which much of people's time is spent and where many of the structures, routines, memories and practices that shape their lives are established. The small space people call home is a kind of drawing together of things from a number of different times and places. The furniture, food, books, TV programmes and other things that define a home reflect a series of connections. This network links home to other places, towns, regions and countries, global supply chains and satellites up in space as well as things closer to home, such as libraries, supermarkets, allotments and schools. There will probably be elements of distant memories and long-departed relatives as well as traces of recent finger marks or the last meal you ate. In this sense, the home is a site where many things meet from across time and space. It is in this convergence that people come to develop a '**geographical imagination**' of the world (Gregory, 1994); that is, to be able to see the flows and connections between places, their similarities and differences, and also the locations of centres of power and inequality.

Geographical imagination
A way of thinking about the world that is intrinsically spatial and acknowledges that all processes are embedded within relations across space. For example, it is impossible to think about a concept such as 'home' without thinking about the other places and times to which it connects.

This chapter explores a range of concepts and ideas that inform this understanding of the world, recognising the central importance of space and place in how people and their environment are interconnected. Using this geographical imagination to think about home, the everyday, the nearby, and faraway places as well, this chapter draws on one of the favourite tools of the geographer – the map. Maps enable us to think about what is meant by space and place and how they are related, their connection to the making of home and how they provide its sense of meaning. This chapter aims to consider ideas about power that may lead to a rethinking of what the mapping of space represents. This is set within a context of globalisation – that is, a world of increased connections and movements across space. Following on from this, the chapter considers home in the context of global inequality and asks why some homes are poorer than others, drawing connections between how power and historical and social influences converge on different homes in different ways. The movement of people between homes, within countries and internationally, often driven by inequality, has led to new thinking about the home as a concept that is not always fixed and stable. A migrant may belong to more than one home, for example. In tension with this idea of home as something fluid is the idea that it is the centre of identity and belonging. The final section explores representations of landscapes that have often been used to recreate and reinforce a sense of home as attached to a particular place. Yet, even this emotional dimension of the geographical imagination of home is something that can be questioned.

This chapter will:

- explore geographical imagination and the impact of power on representations of space and place
- begin to critique the use of maps as a way of representing both the physical and social world
- examine particular case studies, including inequality in development, transnational migration and the representation of landscape.

- Section 1, 'Remapping home', outlines the key geographical concepts of 'space' and 'place' and explores the ways in which meanings become attached to place and how power is also implicated in these meanings. The example of mapmaking is used to illustrate the relationship between power, meaning and place.

- Section 2, 'Geographies of inequality', begins to consider the theme of inequality in more detail and how the historical legacies of colonialism and the continued influences of globalisation create inequalities across the globe and between homes.

- Section 3, 'Geographies of mobility', considers the role of migration and the mobility of people in challenging the idea of home, and how, despite this, there is still an enduring sense that home provides an important sense of attachment and belonging.

- Section 4, '"Seeing" home', highlights how this sense of belonging and attachment is also central to the use of landscape in symbolising a sense of home, and how a broader sense of 'homeland' has become a significant and powerful way in which a sense of home has been linked to nation.

1 Remapping home

Using a geographical imagination, space and place are two key concepts that enable us to think about what we mean by 'home'. The idea of place is often closely associated with feelings of belonging or attachment as expressed in phrases such as 'a sense of place' or feeling 'in one's place'. Place, then, is not simply a specific location within a larger space (a village within a country, for example), but rather is something that combines our sense of self, our day-to-day activities and the spaces in which these things are played out. People imagine that other people in their town, for example, are likely to share similar practices: getting up in the morning, going to school or work, maybe going to the pub or a restaurant in the evening, shopping or playing sport at the weekend. It is the repetition of these everyday practices, and the relationship between the people involved, that constructs a particular place that feels familiar, one where memories are located. A sense of place is therefore specific to a particular context and point in time.

People invest different meanings in particular places; that is, they have an understanding of what a place should be used for, by whom and at what time of day. A religious service would not generally be conducted in a pub, for example, although some people may disagree. Therefore there is, or can be, a contestation of place, as different users may argue about what a particular place can be used for and by whom. The strength of these arguments stems from a sense of attachment to places, from the local to the national scale. Conflicts such as that which began in the Ukraine in 2014 or debates on independence such as in the regions of the United Kingdom reflect how divisive these arguments about belonging and place can be.

Space may seem like an overarching category within which places are found but, while entwined, the two are different entities. A place without people and practices, memories and attachment is just space! Some social scientists suggest that processes of globalisation in the 1980s (discussed over the following sections) began to drive a separation of space and place to such an extent that the world was becoming 'placeless' as people and things could now be unattached and moved globally (see e.g. Harvey, 1990). The increasing ties between countries, the superseding of states by multinational companies, and the speed of transport and telecommunications led researchers such as

Emberley to argue that 'the possibility of space being invested with human meaning, such that it could be interpreted as "place", has evaporated' (1989, p. 754).

However, more recent research has argued that, in fact, place has not disappeared. Nationalism, for example, as a feeling of attachment to place, seems as important as ever in the 21st century, as you will read about in the next chapter. Massey (2005) argues that ideas about what place means within contemporary life needs to be rethought: from place as something settled, enclosed and coherent to place as a meeting point or the intersection of activity, both local and global. The relationship between local and global may seem complicated and indistinct, but the numerous complex interconnections of globalisation still link places together. Massey's ideas will be explored later in the chapter using the example of home.

1.1   Mapping space and place

Topography
The detailed description of the surface features of an area of land. This would usually include capturing the height, depth and undulation of land – referred to as relief – as well as geological features such as lakes and mountains, environmental features such as marsh, heathland or woodland, and constructed features such as buildings and other structures.

Maps are a means of capturing space and defining the boundaries of place. These representations of space and place provide a sense of which countries are distant and which are near, as well as their **topography** and the landscape. Maps of towns can show a particular order – the way traffic should flow, for example – or places of interest. However, a more critical analysis of maps highlights that a great deal is not shown. A territorial map such as Figure 4.1 does not show the interconnections between countries; it does not show how the borders of Europe have shifted and changed over time; it does not take into account nomadic movement across land such as that undertaken by the Sami or the Roma; it does not show how people feel about the country they live in or the connections they may have with other countries.

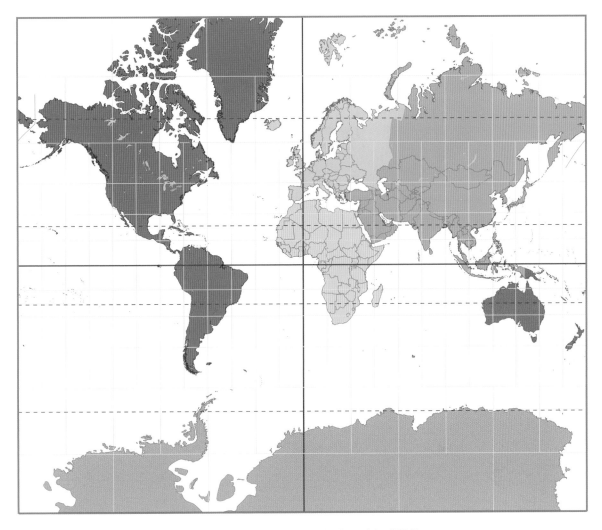

Figure 4.1   The Mercator map of the world (originally designed in 1569)

Ryan (1996) has argued that, in fact, maps represent much more than territory or topography. Their construction is underpinned by the cartographer's or planner's particular ways of seeing the world, which are influenced by their dominant culture. Therefore, power is embedded in maps: the power to ignore some places of interest while highlighting others; to claim land as belonging to one country; or to make some communities or people invisible. The understanding of the role of power in mapmaking (and of the distortions created by depicting a three-dimensional world on a two-dimensional map) led to new representations such as the Peters map (Figure 4.2).

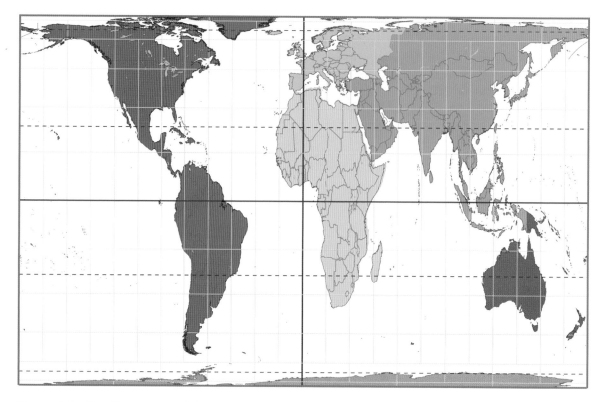

Figure 4.2   The Peters map of the world (1973)

Activity 1

How is the Peters map in Figure 4.2 different from the Mercator map in Figure 4.1?

Discussion

The Mercator map (1569) is a standard representation of the world designed for navigation. Yet in trying to represent a three-dimensional globe on a flat plane it distorts the size of countries, making the more powerful countries (Europe and the United States) appear to have bigger land masses than they actually have in comparison with larger, but often less powerful, countries, which appear smaller. The Peters map (1973) tried to create an equal-area projection so that countries are shown in the correct proportion to each other. It has been used in particular by non-government and development organisations to highlight the relationship between power and inequality in the world, and this has led to some criticism of it.

Other maps have tried to create a more balanced depiction, such as the Robinson map (1963) in Figure 4.3. While it still has some distortion because it is not an equal-area projection, it does present a better proportion of countries in the northern hemisphere and is being increasingly used, for example, in schools.

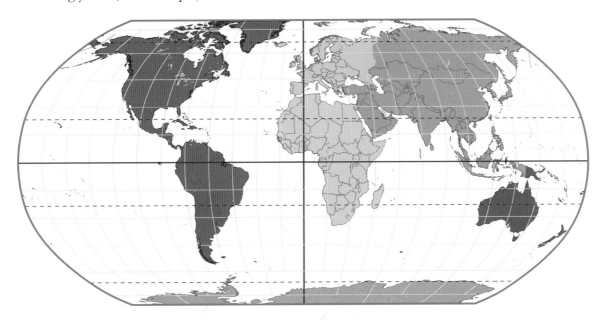

Figure 4.3   The Robinson map of the world (1963)

Adding to these debates about how space is represented is the impact of globalisation; that is, the need to capture contemporary global flows and interconnections of people, money, technology, images and ideas that move around the world, often bypassing neighbouring countries. Mapping global flows reveals shifting ideas about what is local. Figure 4.4 highlights how countries are interconnected by flows of money; in this case, money earned by migrants in one country that is then sent back to their home. As this map shows, countries that no longer share a border, or that are unequal in terms of size and wealth, can now have strong ties because of the movement of money and people that may not have existed in the past.

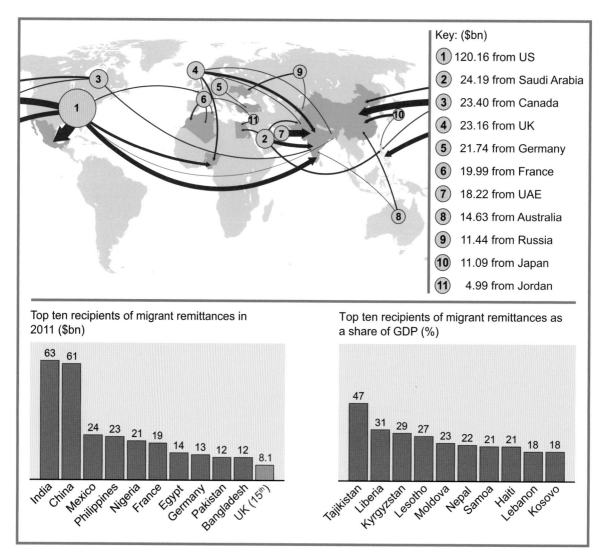

Figure 4.4   'Where the money goes'. This map shows where some of the $500bn of remittance money, sent home by migrants across the world in 2011, went (Rogers and Scruton, 2013)

1.2   The role of power in shaping place: the work of de Certeau and Massey

Even with these new ideas about what it is possible to map, there are still some limitations. For example, going back to the earlier discussion of place, thinking of 'home [as] where one feels oneself "in one's place"' (Cosgrove, 2000, p. 732), how can this capture the processes that create and maintain a sense of home in the midst of global flows and interconnections? More specifically, there is a need to understand 'the social struggles and negotiations through which the personal sense of home place is realized' (Cosgrove, 2000, p. 732). Just as with the creation of maps, understanding how a sense of home is created involves thinking about the role of power in shaping and defining that place. Two influential social science thinkers who have focused on these questions are de Certeau (1925–1986) and Massey (1944–).

Figure 4.5   Michel de Certeau and Doreen Massey

De Certeau was interested in a wider space of home and belonging – the city – and how the everyday practices of residents could disrupt local authorities' ordered planning. His work is useful to consider here because it draws attention to the way in which a particular place can be understood in different ways. This understanding is subject to power struggles and, to this end, place can remain unsettled and contested, an idea that also presents a challenge to the process of mapping. In his famous essay, 'Walking in the city' (de Certeau, 1984), he draws a comparison between the way in which cities are mapped out by planners in a legible and ordered manner, like the mapmakers noted earlier, and the way people living in those same cities experience and shape them, challenging the idealised view of the planner. De Certeau begins by drawing attention to the 'solar eye' of the planner that allows them to look down on a city, 'like a god' (de Certeau, 1984, p. 92). He conveys this sense of power by opening the essay with a description of a view from the top of the former World Trade Center in Manhattan, New York:

> Beneath the haze stirred up by the winds, the urban island, a sea in the middle of the sea, lifts up the skyscrapers over Wall Street, sinks down at Greenwich, then rises again to the crests of Midtown, quietly passes over Central Park and finally undulates off into the distance beyond Harlem.
>
> (de Certeau, 1984, p. 91)

Figure 4.6   The view looking north from the south of Manhattan, New York

For de Certeau, this view of the city is like the Mercator map (as shown in Figure 4.1): a picture or representation of the city space made by, and for, those who have designed and built it, that enables it to be navigated. It is a strategy for shaping the city within a fixed and static understanding of space. However, he argues that to view the city from this position is to misunderstand how people actually experience and use it. Residents make sense of the city by weaving places together with their associated memories as they walk through its streets. These continual, daily movements of people are what create and shape city space, giving it meaning and, in turn, a sense of place, a sense of home. So in his work de Certeau is drawing attention to how power can be used to create particular places, not necessarily with negative intentions, but also how that power can be subverted or represented differently.

Like de Certeau, Massey (1993, 2005) emphasises the role of power in creating a sense of place, including a sense of home. The focus of her argument challenges the common understanding of globalisation as a universally powerful and unstoppable force that is leading to a 'shrinking world'. This is a phenomenon that has also been described by the geographer Harvey (1990) as 'time–space compression', where practices such as air travel, email and international news media have created a sense that space has shrunk and is now dominated by the demands of time. You may feel that life has become faster! Massey argues that time–space compression is commonly, and, in her view, wrongly, opposed to a sense of place that is inaccurately cast as local, fixed and isolated. For Massey, the local and global are much more intertwined than this, and she makes two specific points.

The first point is that the time–space compression associated with globalisation is not a force that sweeps around the world, but rather that 'some are more in charge of it than others; some initiate flows and movement, others don't; some are more on the receiving end of it than others' (Massey, 1993, p. 61). These uneven flows and connections across space create what Massey calls 'power geometry'. Power geometry describes the way that power creates different spatial connections and movements for different groups of people. Apartheid in South Africa would be a extreme example of this, but there are also many everyday laws or expectations that impact people in different, unequal, ways. Importantly, Massey emphasises that, while globalisation might seem like a universal phenomenon in which we are all part of a shrinking world, some groups have more mobility and power than others within these interconnections.

In simple terms, the ability of some to generate or maintain the interconnections of globalisation, such as the transnational professionals discussed in Section 3, 'Geographies of mobility', can impact on a sense of home for others. For example, the decisions by many companies once based in England to outsource manufacturing to other countries, and the impact that has had on communities in the north of England where manufacturing used to take place, results in what Massey has argued is spatial inequality between the south-east and northern regions of the country.

Essentialised
Describing something
as essentialised
indicates that it is
thought of as being
reducible to an essence
of specific, unchanging
and often crude
characteristics. So, for
example, an
essentialised
understanding of
England often includes
characteristics such as
rolling hills and church
steeples set in a 'green
and pleasant land'.

The second point Massey makes, however, is that a localised,
essentialised understanding of place is also problematic. What gives
home its specific character is not an isolated history but its particular
relationship to other places and times (Massey, 1993). A home in
Manchester may be characterised as British by its occupants, but it will
bear the traces of connections to a colonial past and a globalised
present. In this sense Massey also observes a common thread between
space and time in the way that space, like time, should be understood
as a process that is continually changing and unfolding. This idea is
explored further in Section 4 on landscape.

Activity 2

From your understanding of de Certeau and Massey, how is power
implicated in the formation of particular places? For example, think of a
place in your neighbourhood, perhaps a public space such as a park or
town square, or a building such as a library or a business premises. How
is power embedded in that space – in the architecture, in laws governing
its use, in who feels they can access it? How do people contest the use
of that space?

Discussion

Using a town square as an example, often the architecture is designed
to suggest that it is a place of authority. There may be statues or
memorials of important people or events that connect it to the past. The
architecture can be 'monumental'; that is, rather grand in size and
design. There may be bans on particular activities such as 'no ball
games' or 'no drinking'. Such laws are designed to ensure that a space
is used only in particular ways; for example, deterring young people from
playing there allows the space to represent a particular order. But people
can contest these spaces by demonstrating in front of the town hall, or
using it in ways that were not intended, such as skateboarding, for
example.

This kind of geographical analysis of power highlights the level and
types of inequality between people. A town square can demonstrate
inequalities between those who have access to power and those who
do not. At an international level, the same kind of analysis of space
and power leads to an understanding of global inequalities, and why

some homes have more wealth than others, as the next section will examine.

Summary

- This section has defined the key concepts of space and place, arguing that space becomes place when invested with meaning and memory.

- Maps may not provide an objective representation of place but are in fact influenced by power and culture.

- Globalisation, with its associated increase in interconnections and movement around the planet, has destabilised people's understanding of what place is.

- The work of Massey and de Certeau demonstrates how power is implicated in the understanding of place.

2   Geographies of inequality: why some homes are poorer than others

The previous section introduced the role of power in the mapping of places and in the organisation of people's everyday lives. Power is something that is often unequally shared, demarcating difference and having real social and economic impacts. Even intimate spaces such as the home can be marked by unequal social and economic power relations that originate in contemporary and historical factors. For example, within a family home, age and gender can impact on who has the power to make decisions (see Chapter 1). Within the country or nation as home, people from minority backgrounds can be exposed to discrimination from dominant, more powerful, groups, and as a result their homes are more likely to be poorer than others. To explore these interconnections between power and inequality and their impact on home, this section will focus on how geographies of inequality have emerged in the context of the relationship between countries.

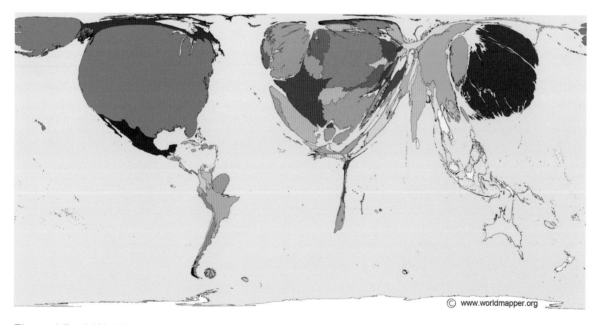

Figure 4.7   A Worldmapper map of national income with territory size showing the proportion of all gross national income, in US dollars, that is attributed to that place (SASI Group and Newman, 2006)

As noted earlier, maps can not only be used to highlight where countries begin and end, but can also provide a way of representing different relationships between places. For example, maps can illustrate where wealth and poverty are located globally. Figure 4.7 highlights the inequality between countries through distorting territory size according to gross national income, or, more simply, how much a country earns. Richer countries appear bloated while poorer ones become thin in comparison. What is invisible on this map, however, is the processes of economic development that led to this inequality, which ultimately generates inequality between homes.

From the 1980s, along with increasing globalisation, a particular approach to development known as 'neoliberalism' began to be adopted internationally (Hanlin and Brown, 2013). Like many of the key concepts in the social sciences, different disciplines will have their own definition and use of terms. In development geography, neoliberalism is used to describe a reduced role for governments in directing economic output, often known as deregulation of economies, and an increased role for the private sector in providing goods and services that are, in theory, driven by consumer demand. Wealth should then 'trickle down' to those with less resources.

Some would argue that with neoliberal development has come a reduction in poverty in poorer countries. The World Bank (2013) reports that, since 1990, the percentage of people living in extreme poverty globally has been halved. Others, however, question these outcomes, arguing that extreme poverty, that is, living on less than US $1.25 a day, still exists in many parts of the world. And relative poverty that is related to inequality in different contexts persists even in countries designated as part of the **Global North**, such as the UK and the United States. For example, in the UK it was estimated during 2008–09 that 23 per cent of the population, or 13.5 million people, were living in poverty (Rowntree Foundation, 2014). In addition, while poverty may have declined in some countries, it is argued that inequality has increased. Oxfam (2014) has reported that almost half of the world's wealth is held by just one per cent of the population.

This inequality has an obvious impact on homes: not only a growing disparity between those with high and low incomes, but also a disparity in the ability to access education, healthcare and affordable housing, as discussed in the previous chapters. This compounds poverty and other forms of discrimination such as gender inequality. As a result increased attention has been given to the negative impacts of inequality on society. It is argued that inequality creates a generational cycle whereby people who are unable to access resources, for example, education, will not be able to develop the capacity to access a better livelihood in the

Global North
After the Second World War, the world began to be seen as divided into 'developed' (wealthy) and 'undeveloped' (poor) countries. Today, the terms 'Global North' and 'Global South' are used, which still geographically divides the world into wealthier and poorer regions but removes the ideas of an ideal or 'Western' state of development that countries must strive to obtain. It is important to note that these are not necessarily contiguous geographical spaces but rather conceptual divisions. Australia, for example, as a wealthy country, would be considered part of the Global North, even though it is in the southern hemisphere.

future (Sen, 1992). This has led to geographies of inequality at different scales, as homes, neighbourhoods, regions and countries can be said to be in relationships of inequality. For example, the eastern boroughs of London such as Tower Hamlets and Newham have higher levels of poverty when compared with more prosperous boroughs in the west of the city, such as Kensington and Chelsea or Richmond-upon-Thames (Figure 4.8).

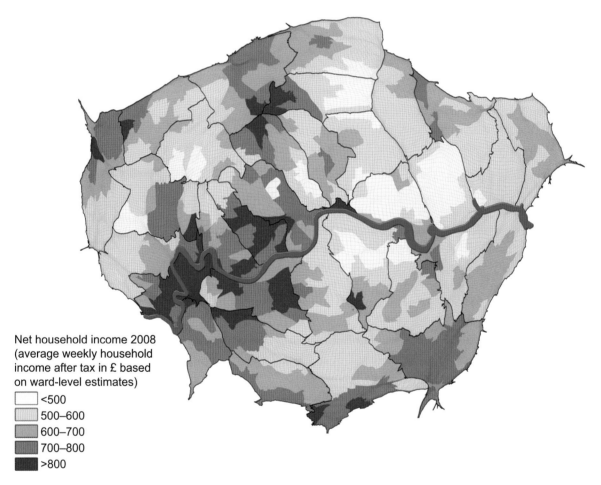

Net household income 2008
(average weekly household
income after tax in £ based
on ward-level estimates)

☐	<500
▨	500–600
▨	600–700
▨	700–800
■	>800

Figure 4.8   Net household income for London boroughs in 2008, with each grid cell resized according to the number of people living in that area (Hennig and Dorling, 2011)

The north of England has, in general, lower levels of income and higher unemployment than London and the south-east region of the country. The relationship between countries within regions of the Global North and Global South is also unequal, with the Global South marked by extreme poverty and lack of access to global markets.

However, these divisions of inequality as seen in Figures 4.7 and 4.8 are not so neat in reality. There are pockets of wealth within poorer boroughs in the UK and pockets of poverty in the wealthiest boroughs. In countries in the Global South there can be immense wealth (Figure 4.9), as well as examples of extreme poverty in countries in the Global North, such as the UK (Figure 4.10). So it is possible to argue that the Global North and South are intertwined through economic relationships, with overlapping pockets of wealth and poverty within each other's geographic sphere.

Figure 4.9   The 27-storey home in Mumbai of Mukesh Ambani, one of India's wealthiest businessmen

As an example of Massey's power geometry, one argument is that the global economy is dominated by the neo-liberal development approach because it favours particular groups that drive its continuation. Many of the protest movements that emerged following the banking crisis of 2007 pointed to statistics showing that those who already had a high degree of power through economic accumulation were able to consolidate it, and the 'trickle-down' of wealth had not occurred (*The Economist*, 2011). The offshoring of business, especially manufacturing,

Figure 4.10   A garden shed conversion into a home in London

to those countries that had cheaper wage bills, created wealth and employment in those countries, positively increased income in homes there, but caused unemployment in former centres of power such as the north of England and the United States.

Another factor that has created contemporary inequality between households is how power has been deployed in the past. For example, taking advantage of geographical location and access to resources such as coal, Britain was at the forefront of the Industrial Revolution from the 18th century. It used its economic and military power to maintain an empire whose resources could be used for its own economic growth while disrupting the economic and social organisation that underpinned households in colonised countries. This system of relations between states, which established a more powerful group of countries at the centre of world affairs and left poorer, less powerful countries at the periphery (Wallerstein, 2004), was maintained after countries gained independence in the 20th century. Countries of the Global North were able to maintain their comparative advantage through having already developed a level of technological innovation, as well as maintaining control over organisations such as the World Bank that set the rules for international trade.

Inequality can also be evident in social relations within the home. It could be argued that women have benefited in some ways from neoliberal development, gaining access to employment and income, for example, which has increased social mobility. However, social scientists have highlighted ongoing inequalities perpetuated in particular representations, and a gendered division of labour in the home where women's work, particularly domestic labour, has been devalued (Longhurst, 2008; see Chapter 1). Take the case of Tendai, a young woman living in Zimbabwe:

> Her day starts at 4 a.m., when, to fetch water, she carries a thirty-litre tin to a borehole about eleven kilometers from her home. She walks barefoot and is home by 9 a.m. She eats a little and proceeds to fetch firewood until midday. She cleans the utensils from the family's morning meal and sits preparing sadza [porridge] for the family's lunch. After lunch and cleaning of the dishes, she wanders in the hot sun until early evening, fetching wild vegetables for supper before making the evening trip for water. Her day ends at 9 p.m., after she has prepared supper and put her younger brothers and sisters to sleep.
>
> (Waring, 1999, p. 13)

According to predominant international economic accounting methods, such as gross national income, Tendai does not work. Similarly, women in industrialised countries have argued that their own domestic labour needs to be taken into account to address inequalities in the home.

Activity 3

This section has highlighted how unequal relationships in the international system have led to inequality between homes. Do you think that wealthier countries have an obligation to reduce inequality both locally and globally as part of an ethos of justice? Does everyone have a right to a living wage and secure home, even if it means that others have to give up some of their wealth?

Discussion

Questions of justice are contentious and continually debated by politicians, philosophers and social scientists, so the answers to these questions will depend on your own beliefs and values. Rather than attempt to give a definitive answer, it is more important to be aware of your values and what influences them. In reflecting on your answers to the questions in this activity, take a few minutes to think about what influences your values. Is it particular media commentators, family members or political philosophies? Ask yourself, where do their values that inform their opinions come from? Why do we accept certain opinions as being more valid than others, and is this also a question of power?

Another controversial issue often debated in the media and politics is migration. People have always moved from areas of poverty and deprivation to those places where they could find work or better opportunities. Mapping these flows of migration is another way of observing inequalities between places, as the next section will examine.

Summary

- This section has discussed inequality in the relationship between countries and how this has led to inequality between homes.

- This inequality has both historical and contemporary influences, such as colonialism and globalisation.

- Massey's notion of 'power geometry' can be applied to the argument that a particular model of development (neoliberalism) associated with globalisation is maintained because it favours particular powerful groups.

- Maps may highlight areas of general poverty and inequality, but these areas can also be entwined with pockets of wealth, and vice versa.

3   Geographies of mobility: why some homes are more mobile than others

In the 20th century, when countries such as the UK needed labour to rebuild after the Second World War, people from former colonies were encouraged to migrate from the 'periphery' to the 'centre'. In recent years, others have moved to escape poverty or conflict. This movement of people has caused researchers to rethink ideas of home. Diasporic communities, transnational mobility, and the second and third generations of migrant families all challenge the idea that home is related to a specific physical place connected to a nation state (see Chapter 5).

The following is the work itinerary of an Australian transnational professional working for a European telecommunications company, who, while based in his 'home' in Australia, spent 11 out of 12 months working in Asia for six years.

> Stephen lived in Vietnam, New Zealand, Taiwan, Malaysia, and Sri Lanka for periods of more than four months; he worked in China, India, Thailand, Myanmar, Indonesia, Singapore and South Korea for periods from one to four weeks. When back in Australia he would keep in daily contact via phone with offices in Asia and made more than fifty trips within the region. He chose to 'slow down' and take a more sedentary role when he decided to begin a family.
>
> (Butcher, 2011, p. 25)

As noted in the previous section, new forms of transnational business activities have led to increasing emphasis on the off-shore relocation of manufacturing and other industries. This has seen an increase in the number of skilled professionals moving globally to manage those businesses and provide a link between head and regional offices. However, while this movement was initially dominated by professionals from industrialised, European and North American countries, more and more professionals from countries considered to be in the Global South are now also relocating, indicative of shifting power in the global economy (Raghuram and Erel, 2014). India's relocation of its information technology and financial service sector technicians, sales staff and management teams to countries in Europe, North America and other parts of Asia is a case in point, as is the movement of Chinese businesspeople to African countries (Mohan, 2013).

One of the key geographical questions concerning the impact of this mobility is whether it is creating a decline in a sense of belonging to a nation state as home. Huntington (2004) famously described mobile elites as 'dead souls' with little feelings of commitment to their native land. Dual or flexible citizenship (Ong, 2006), and the ideas of bi-national identity and that feelings of home can be removed from a particular territory, seem to contradict the idea that people belong to a particular place, with a specific culture that influences their everyday practices and values.

Home, as noted already in this chapter, is often defined as a place of birth, a place of citizenship, or a place of belonging and familiarity where memories are created. However, just as ideas of place have become, in theory, increasingly unsettled as a result of globalisation and mobility, so too have social scientists seen 'home' as something more fluid, 'a space in-becoming' (Nowicka, 2007, p. 73) or 'in process' (McKay, 2006, p. 200). This idea is supported by work indicating there can be tension and contradictory feelings in attempts to define 'home' during periods of cultural change such as migration. A study by Nowicka (2007) with highly mobile professionals working for an international agency suggested that, for her participants, home was no longer a fixed location. As she states, 'I do not assume that home is a stable physical place where domestic life is realised nor that home is a secure and closed territory [as in the nation-state]' (Nowicka, 2007, p. 70).

This presumes that a sense of belonging is made more difficult when people migrate, but the re-negotiation of home under conditions of globalisation is often more complicated. There are increasingly complex interconnections linking places together. Relationships between places are being redefined as they stretch across borders, shifting the idea of home as a place that is settled and unchanging, as Al-Ali and Koser argue (2002, pp. 7–8, their italics):

> Despite the unsettling of previously rooted and fixed notions of home, people engaged in transnational practices might express an uneasiness, a sense of fragmentation, tension and even pain. ...

> Fear, danger, the unknown, foreign, alien places and traditions, unfamiliar faces and habits are all part of that which is *not home*.

What Al-Ali and Koser (2002) are suggesting is that home is not only physical, made up of objects and everyday activities such as washing up, or eating and sleeping, but it also has an emotional dimension. People become attached to places. It must feel like home, embedded in memories of the familiar, family and friends, where the landscape and built environment feel comfortable, where you can just be yourself, as opposed to a context that generates uncertainty and threat. This definition is similar to Cosgrove's (2000, p. 732) argument noted earlier that 'home [is] where one feels oneself "in one's place"'.

While it could be argued that home is no longer necessarily related to a place, many migrants, including highly mobile professionals such as Stephen mentioned earlier, can also take their home with them. Re-placing home, reaffirming existing boundaries or re-finding new ones, and moving between two or more homes are all part of adapting to change. Expatriates may claim belonging to former homes where they used to live, sometimes coloured by nostalgia, and to new homes that can contain markers of both locations. Being nomadic today can mean being able to recreate home anywhere, through carrying out the same routines anywhere in the world, like having a coffee at the same international coffee chain in any major city in the world, or maintaining close family relationships using new chat technologies such as Skype. The transnational professionals in Nowicka's (2007) study, for example, organised their homes around people and familiar objects rather than a location.

So while globalisation does involve processes of money and companies moving around the world, for the individuals driving these corporations, place and home still matter, with former homes sometimes being recreated in a new location or new homes being created with elements of past ones. These complex interconnections between mobile populations, global flows of capital, companies and other countries can be seen in the formation of what has become known as the world wide web of Chinese business. A study by Ong (2006) found that Hong Kong businesspeople, facing the political uncertainty of the return of Hong Kong to the Chinese in 1997, began to apply for citizenship of other countries. She refers to this as a form of flexible citizenship, where Hong Kong businesspeople sought to work in China but maintain citizenship elsewhere. As part of this strategy, they began to invest in homes for their families in North America, Europe and Australia but also to continue to invest in business enterprises in Asia. There is flexibility in the family as a result of this mobility, with parents, predominantly fathers, often travelling while the family lived elsewhere. In this sense, citizenship, and the idea of home that goes with it, has mutated and become more flexible.

Activity 4

What do you think are the 'power geometries', as Massey has described them, involved in this movement of transnational professionals?

Discussion

Remember the definition of power geometry:

'Power geometry is used to describe the way that power creates different spatial connections and movements for different groups of people. Importantly, it emphasises that while globalisation might seem like a universal phenomenon in which we are all part of a shrinking world, some groups have more power than others within these interconnections.'

For transnational professionals, it seems that they can move much more easily around the globe. For example, Melissa (co-author of this chapter) was born in Australia but has two passports, Australian and British, so does not have to worry about immigration in the UK or the EU. Trade agreements between countries sometimes enable the movement of people associated with business but restrict the movement of other people, such as undocumented workers. Questions of inequality and justice are reflected in this movement and the legal regimes that govern it. Undocumented workers may have been forced to migrate due to a loss of livelihood that was beyond their control, or that was actually created by models of economic organisation implemented by the country they are trying to migrate to. Mexican migration into the United States as a result of the North American Free Trade Agreement is one example of this power geometry.

The idea that home is something fluid and flexible seems counter-intuitive when observing the material objects and the practices de Certeau talks about that mark out maps of home, and the real feelings of warmth when thinking about places to which we belong. So it is important to note that, in much of the research with migrants in general, home still matters.

Landscapes provide illustrations of the ways in which an idea or sense of home is important and the final section turns to these representations.

Summary

- This section has explored how ideas about home can be contested by processes of migration and the movement of people globally.

- People can maintain connections to more than one home.

- Home can also be remade or relocated. However, while home may seem like a flexible idea, for many people it is still an important marker of identity and belonging.

4   'Seeing' home: representing spaces of home

The previous section touched on the idea that, while home might sometimes be experienced in mobile or unsettled ways, place still matters. The landscape or the environment provides a setting where this sense of home is embedded; what might be called 'homelands'. As the geographer Tuan (2004, p. 164) puts it:

> [we] can extrapolate 'home' far beyond the directly experienceable – house, neighbourhood and towns – to such large spaces as region and nation-state. A whole country, even one of continental size, can then become home, or homeland – and homeland, even more than home, is a guarantor of security and nurture.

This idea of a whole country as home is something that is central to the meaning of nationhood. It is expressed through a range of rituals and symbols, as you will see in the next chapter.

This section focuses on landscape and its connection to national identity. In the introduction to his historical account, *The Making of the English Landscape*, Hoskins (2013 [1955], p. 14) notes that: 'the English Landscape itself, to those who know how to read it aright, is the richest historical record we possess'. This quote, and Hoskins' pioneering work on landscape history more broadly, describes a particular understanding of landscape that is deeply embedded in the concept of a national identity. Yet there is something more to Hoskins' statement than that: it is the idea that landscape, as a spatial concept, is something that can also be read like a text, painting or photograph.

The distinction between landscape as something spatial and as something textual has been historically blurred, especially since the 18th century when the concept of landscape gained particular popularity in European literature and art. At this time it was increasingly fashionable among the British aristocracy to display their growing colonial wealth and to have their land (as well as their paintings) as models of 'the picturesque'. While alluding to the 'wild' and 'natural', the picturesque landscape was, in fact, governed by very particular rules and norms of composition outlined by figures such as William Gilpin, who saw his role as 'examining landscape by the rules

Figure 4.11   A northern English rural landscape

of picturesque beauty' (Gilpin, 2004 [1786], p. 23). These ideas were heavily influenced by the work of the 17th century French painter Claude Lorrain and later by the works of 18th century English painters such as Gainsborough and Turner, as well as the fashionable 'country house' garden designs of Lancelot 'Capability' Brown and others.

Bearing this historical context in mind, and the slippage between landscape as something spatial and as a text that can be read, 'landscape can be thought of as both something seen *and* a "way of seeing" the world … associated in particular with the visualisation of relationships between culture and nature' (Wylie, 2007, p. 55, emphasis in original).

However, this 'way of seeing', like geographical imagination, is not an unproblematic idea. It is a 'refined' way of seeing, informed by aristocratic landowners, collectors of paintings and readers of literature at a time when around 50 per cent of the English adult population was illiterate (Vincent, 1993). In other words, it is an idealised vision of English landscape that is selective in *what* and *who* is seen. As the art critic John Berger observed: 'Sometimes a landscape seems to be less a setting for the life of its inhabitants than a curtain behind which their struggles, achievements and accidents take place' (cited in Cosgrove, 1984, p. 271). It has subsequently been argued that this privileged view of landscape, or 'gaze' as it is often termed, served to marginalise the poor, non-white ethnic groups and women, who were largely absent from representations of landscape at this time (Dorrian and Rose, 2003).

Figure 4.12   Stourhead Gardens, Wiltshire

Figure 4.13   *Landscape with Jacob and Laban and Laban's Daughters* (Claude Lorrain, 1654)

These kinds of landscape paintings can reinforce ideas about who does and who does not belong in certain spaces. They contain and reflect relations of power. Disputes over the 'gentrification' of cities via new and expensive apartments, and the ways in which that can price 'local' people out, provide a contemporary example of this.

The argument about representation takes us back to de Certeau (1984) and his idea of the tussle between the power of officials to render a landscape in a particular way, and the everyday practices of people who use that space. It is apparent that landscape is a contested concept, moving almost interchangeably between taking on a role as a text that is telling us something about how we define home, and a physical space that creates real emotions of belonging and attachment. It is simultaneously embedded in ideas of nature and culture, and it is contested for framing a particular, selective view.

The power of this concept of landscape is precisely in the way it serves to link a number of things together in the geographical imagination: place, memory, identity and feelings of home. This is perhaps why landscape and the idea of a national homeland have an enduring relationship, creating stories of a particular sense of place as Rose (1995, pp. 106–7) argues, using England and Englishness as an example:

> The search for a symbol of the nation thus turned to the countryside of the south of England. The soft hills, small villages around a green, winding lanes and church steeples of the English southern counties came to represent England and all the qualities the culturally dominant classes desired. ... this sense of place suggested that the relationship between humans and nature had reached a balance through the centuries; it was shown as a deeply historical landscape. Finally, this landscape was argued to stand for all England. It was this image which stood for the country as a whole.

While the 'soft hills' and village greens of southern England convey one sense of home, the Highlands of northern Scotland have most often been used to tell the stories of that nation. These representations are based on images of mountains and wilderness, evoking a timeless and unchanging landscape. If there are living things represented in these idealised depictions, they are often solitary human figures or animals. As Jamie (2008, pp. 4–7) has argued though, these 'theatrically empty places [are] also contested, [and] politicised … For a long time, the wild land was a working place, whether you were a hunter-gatherer, a crofter, a miner'.

Figure 4.14   *The Monarch of the Glen* (Landseer, 1851)

One of the most commonly evoked areas of Scottish landscape in these stories of home and national identity is the Cairngorm Mountains. While these have featured in a number of historical literary and artistic depictions, their significance increased with the establishment of the Cairngorms as a National Park in 2003. The campaign for this area to be granted such a status can be traced back to an initial public campaign in *The Scots Magazine* in 1928 that was part of 'an irresistible push for the democratization and demarcation of the Cairngorms as a recreational space for the nation' (Lorimer, 2003, p. 204). A key issue for this initial campaign, and part of the reason that it became so protracted, was that it challenged the area's status as an 'aristocratic sporting retreat', and instead sought to establish 'claims to common ownership through the idea of a "national heritage"' (Lorimer, 2003, p. 204). This too shows how power is contested in the efforts of competing stakeholders to 'remap' the social and cultural meanings attached to the landscape of the Cairngorms.

Figure 4.15 'Homecoming Scotland', 2014

Today the Cairngorms, and the Highlands region more broadly, have come to represent a sense of homeland used extensively in reinforcing stories of Scottishness, as the marketing material from Visit Scotland in Figure 4.15 shows. Like the 'soft hills' of southern England, the landscape of the Scottish Highlands has many different stories of home attached to it. These stories can be read using a geographical imagination, which entails asking questions about how power and inequality, attachment and identity are embedded in different and contested ideas of home.

Summary

- This section has explored the historical development of landscape in defining and symbolising a sense of national 'homeland' and identity.

- It has considered the idea that landscape is not just something that is seen, but is also a 'way of seeing' that creates contested and selective views.

- Landscape is a powerful concept that links place, attachment, identity and a sense of home.

Conclusion

This chapter has used home as a means to explore a geographical way of understanding the world. Space and place are central concepts to this perspective, as is the relationship between people and their environment. The idea of a geographical imagination helps reveal the power relationships that underpin ideas about home and how our homes are interconnected to other people, places, regions and institutions.

Maps were used to visualise and explore these relationships, also highlighting that 'official' representations present a particular view of the world that can be contested. De Certeau used the example of city planning, while Massey argued that globalisation, rather than being a natural phenomenon, has been generated and maintained by those with power. Inequality between and within homes can be seen in the geographies of uneven development that has left some much poorer than others. Inequality is a result of lack of power, and contemporary forms of inequality, such as the difference in economic development between countries marked as part of the Global North or Global South, can have their origins of inequalities in the past.

Migration creates new ideas about home as something that can be fluid and flexible rather than static and unchanging. The transnational professionals discussed in this chapter were able to recreate new 'homes' but also still feel attached to other places.

Finally, the discussion on the representation of home as landscape highlights again that home not only consists of material objects but also evokes emotional attachment. Just as with the maps used to navigate borders, cities, countries and regions, power is evident in how depictions of landscapes can make invisible the reality of others who also call a place 'home'.

References

Al-Ali, N. and Koser, K. (2002) 'Transnationalism, international migration and home', in Al-Ali, N. and Koser, K. (eds) *New Approaches to Migration? Transnational Communities and the Transformation of Home*, London and New York, Routledge, pp. 1–14.

Butcher, M. (2011) *Managing Cultural Change: Reclaiming Synchronicity in a Mobile World*, Farnham, Ashgate.

Cosgrove, D. (1984) *Social Formation and Symbolic Landscape*, London, Croom Helm.

Cosgrove, D. (2000) 'Sense of place', in Johnstone, R., Gregory, D., Pratt, G. and Watts. M. (eds) *The Dictionary of Human Geography*, Oxford, Blackwell.

De Certeau, M. (1984) *The Practice of Everyday Life*, Oakland, CA, University of California Press.

Dorrian, M. and Rose, G. (2003) (eds) *Deterritorialisations … Revisioning Landscapes and Politics*, London, Black Dog Publishing.

Economist, The (2011) 'The 99 percent', *The Economist*, 26 October [Online]. Available at www.economist.com/ blogs/dailychart/2011/10/income-inequality-america (Accessed 20 May 2014).

Emberley, P. (1989) 'Places and stories: the challenge of technology', *Social Research*, vol. 56, no. 3, pp. 741–85.

Gilpin, W. (2004 [1786]) 'Observations, relative chiefly to picturesque beauty, made in the Year 1772, on several parts of England; particularly the mountains, and lakes of Cumberland and Westmoreland', in Lavin, C. and Donnachie, I. (eds) *From Enlightenment to Romanticism, Anthology II*, Manchester, Manchester University Press.

Gregory, D. (1994) *Geographical Imaginations*, Oxford, Blackwell.

Hanlin, R. and Brown, W. (2013) 'Contesting development in theory and practice', in Papaioannou, T. and Butcher, M. (eds) *International Development in a Changing World*, London and New York, Bloomsbury Academic, pp. 29–47.

Harvey, D. (1990) *The Condition of Post-Modernity*, Oxford, Blackwell Publishers.

Hennig, B. and Dorling, D. (2011) 'Inequalities in London', *Londonmapper: A Social Atlas of London* [Online]. Available at www.londonmapper.org.uk/ analysis/inequality-in-london/ (Accessed 27 May 2015).

Hoskins, W. (2013 [1955]) *The Making of the English Landscape*, Dorchester, Little Toller Books.

Huntington, S. (2004) 'Dead souls: the denationalisation of the American elite', *The National Interest*, vol. 75, Spring, pp. 5–18.

Jamie, K. (2008) 'A lone enraptured male', *London Review of Books*, vol. 30, no. 5, 6 March, pp. 1–7.

Longhurst, R. (2008) 'Feminism and geography: Gillian Rose', in Hubbard, P., Kitchin, R. and Valentine, G. (eds) *Key Texts in Human Geography*, London, Sage.

Lorimer, H. (2003) 'Telling small stories: spaces of knowledge and the practice of geography', *Transactions of the Institute of British Geographers*, vol. 28, pp. 197–217.

Massey, D. (1993) 'Power-geometry and a progressive sense of place', in Bird, J., Curtis, B., Putnam, T., Robertson, G. and Tickner, L. (eds) *Mapping the Futures: Local Cultures, Global Change*, London, Routledge.

Massey, D. (2005) *On Space*, London, Sage.

McKay, D. (2006) 'Introduction: finding "the field": the problem of locality in a mobile world', *Asia Pacific Journal of Anthropology*, vol. 7, no. 3, pp. 197–202.

Mohan, G. (2013) 'Migrants as agents of South-South cooperation: the case of Chinese in Africa', in Dargin, J. (ed.) *The Rise of the Global South: Philosophical, Geopolitical and Economic Trends of the 21st Century*, London, World Scientific, pp. 283–322.

Nowicka, M. (2007) 'Mobile locations: construction of home in a group of mobile transnational professionals', *Global Networks*, vol. 7, no. 1, pp. 69–86.

Ong, A. (2006) 'Mutations in citizenship', *Theory, Culture and Society*, vol. 23, nos. 2–3, pp. 499–531.

Oxfam (2014) *Working for the Few* [Online]. Available at www.oxfam.org/en/policy/working-for-the-few-economic-inequality (Accessed 16 October 2014).

Raghuram, P. and Erel, U. (2014) 'Migration: changing and connecting places', in Clarke, J. and Woodward, K. (eds) *Introducing the Social Sciences: Understanding Social Lives 2*, Milton Keynes, The Open University.

Rogers, S. and Scruton, P. (2013) 'Where does the money go?', *The Guardian* [Online]. Available at www.theguardian.com/news/datablog/2013/feb/05/remittances-around-world-visualised (Accessed 26 May 2015).

Rose, G. (1995) 'Place and identity: a sense of place', in Massey, D. and Jess, P. (eds) *A Place in the World?*, Oxford, Oxford University Press.

Rowntree Foundation (2014) *Measuring Poverty* [Online]. Available at www.jrf.org.uk/reporting-poverty/facts-figures (Accessed 20 May 2014).

Ryan, S. (1996) *The Cartographic Eye: How Explorers Saw Australia*, Cambridge, Cambridge University Press.

SASI Group and Newman, M. (2006) *National Income* [Online]. Available at www.worldmapper.org/posters/worldmapper_map309_ver5.pdf (Accessed 27 May 2015).

Sen, A. (1992) *Inequality Re-examined*, Oxford, Oxford University Press.

Tuan, Y. (2004) 'Home', in Harrison, S., Pile, S. and Thrift, N. (eds) *Patterned Ground: Entanglements of Nature and Culture*, London, Reaktion Books.

Vincent, D. (1993) *Literacy and Popular Culture: England 1750–1914*, Cambridge, Cambridge University Press.

Wallerstein, I. (2004) *World-systems Analysis: An Introduction*, Durham, NC, Duke University Press.

Waring, M. (1999) *Counting for Nothing: What Men Value and What Women are Worth* (2nd edn), Toronto, University of Toronto Press.

World Bank (2013) *Annual Report: End Extreme Poverty, Promote Shared Prosperity*, Washington, DC, World Bank, [Online]. Available at https://openknowledge.worldbank.org/handle/10986/16091 (Accessed 16 October 2014).

Wylie, J. (2007) *Landscape*, London, Routledge.

Chapter 5

Homelands: the nation, state and nationalisms

by Daniel Conway and Matt Staples

Contents

Introduction

What do you think of when you think about your homeland? It may often be your place of birth, or perhaps the nation or the place where you live. These factual details about a homeland are also combined with emotional feelings, as you saw in the previous chapter. Loyalty to a nation is expressed in terms such as 'the home of the free'. Such phrases are linked to political and social claims about a nation and can inspire deep feelings of pride and belonging. This sense of a homeland suggests something bigger than a house as a 'home', but encompasses the territory of birth or residence.

This chapter addresses the idea of home through a politics and international relations approach. From this perspective, home and homeland, the nation and also the state are the key sources for feelings of belonging, as well as legal belonging. As disciplines, politics and international relations are primarily concerned with political institutions, such as parliaments, and processes, such as elections and international relations conducted by diplomacy or armed conflict. All of these institutions and processes exist in nations and states. For the majority of people in the modern world, their political 'home' is the nation. Many people feel they belong to a 'nation' and, for most, it is where they were born, though migration and diaspora can produce multiple senses of belonging, as you saw in the last chapter.

Patriotism and nationalism are the loyalty, devotion and support for a nation. These emotional and political commitments can be most visible during international sporting events, where many people support and celebrate the successes of their national teams and sports players, and in times of war, when men and women are asked to fight and die for their nation. In travelling abroad, there are frequent reminders of belonging to one state and not others as national boundaries are crossed and people are subject to the international rules and regulations of migration. Travellers carry passports indicating their nationality and return 'home' via passport control at the state border. For many people there is a clear relationship between the state (as a formal political and institutional community) and the nation. For some, however, the relationship between state and the nation is conflictual: they may have their ability to express themselves through a political or cultural belonging to a 'home' or 'nation' denied, or be in conflict with other majority or minority groups who have competing claims to the same home or symbols.

Nations and the states in which they exist, or form a part of, are human constructions and not pre-existing entities. Political scientists are interested in the interplay among different entities in society, nations, states and the international institutions they interact with. This chapter looks at all of these issues in exploring the politics of nation, state and nationalism.

This chapter will explore:

- how nations emerge and national consciousness is produced; how they may be said to exist in people's individual and collective thoughts, in symbols and practices, and in what people say, write and publically express about a nation

- the processes by which states and 'homes' for nations are produced and reproduced

- how these processes are connected to issues of power and inequality in the ability of some to express belonging or claims to a homeland in a political or a cultural sense

- the different claims made by political scientists about the way states and nations interact with each other and how inequalities are dealt with in the international system.

- Section 1, 'What is a nation?', begins by looking at different ways of defining a nation and then moves on to analysing various ways in which a nation is symbolised in everyday life.

- Section 2, 'Nations and the state', explores the relationship between the nation and the state, before looking at the redefining of the national community in South Africa after the end of the apartheid regime.

- Section 3, 'Are all nation claims equal?' includes a case study of the Kurdish nation, which does not have a national 'home state'.

1   What is a nation?

Political theorists debate what constitutes a nation and how nationalist demands should be understood. A nation is sometimes defined as a large group of people with some ethnic, cultural, linguistic and historical links and connections that enable them to be recognised as a distinct grouping. There will, however, be some people who are not part of the recognised group.

Some theorists take the position that nations are modern constructions, while others argue that their origins are older. Gellner (1983) considered **nationalism** as arising from the need of modern societies to be culturally homogeneous. Pre-industrial societies could tolerate high degrees of variation, including ethnic and linguistic diversity. In Gellner's view, pre-industrial societies were hierarchical and communities lived within their local area, often with little knowledge of the broader country in which they lived. By contrast, modern societies are more egalitarian, mobile and homogenous. Nationalism arose out of the pressures and social dislocation resulting from the Industrial Revolution.

Nationalism
The act of identifying with a specific national identity and/or the actions that members of a nation take to achieve self-determination.

Hobsbawm (1983) also argued that nationalism arose during the modern era, broadly speaking from 1789 (the date of the French Revolution) onwards. He viewed it as a process encouraged by elites to legitimise their power amid economic change and the rise of democratic ideas. States and their ruling classes could find in national feeling a means of securing loyalty to replace or supplement traditional bonds, such as loyalty to a ruler or religion. Nationalism, in this account, therefore helped to stabilise elites during the Industrial Revolution and preserve them in the face of democratic demands.

Anderson (1983) portrays the modern nation as an 'imagined community'. By 'imagined', he means that there is an idea that a nation is based on shared histories, outlooks, cultural values and manners that are held in common. However, he argues that this national feeling is entirely 'imagined' and constructed through education, the mass media and political socialisation. From the late 18th century onwards, newspapers allowed communities to be psychologically enlarged while journalists and novelists acted as the carriers of national ideas. Anderson therefore believes nationalism was entirely invented during the modern era and that national histories and traditions are imagined.

Symbols, such as flags, and sporting events are a good example of how individuals and groups can imagine being part of a wider collective when they wear team clothes, and watch, celebrate or commiserate about national events.

The opposite argument is that nations are ancient rather than modern, and that national histories are passed down through the generations. For Smith (1995), nationalism builds on pre-existing ties of kinship, religions and other beliefs. Ethnic groups, or 'ethnies' in Smith's terms, are the basis for nationalist identification on these terms. Smith argues that nations draw on traditions, real or mythical – a shared descent, history and culture. This perspective is termed the 'primordial view of nations', meaning they existed from the beginning. In contrast, modern nationalisms were shaped over time by such factors as wars and the settlement of people by migration.

What nations are and how they emerge are clearly subject to different definitions and claims. At a general level, a nation – and nationalism – can be characterised as a complex blend of cultural, political and economic features. Economic deprivation or recession may lead to an increase in nationalist tensions, as can political or cultural events such as wars and celebrations. States in which different nations exist reveal how nationalist feelings arise, how they become politicised and how they can lead to conflict. In Spain, for example, there have been repeated political demands, sometimes violent, for national self-determination for the Catalan region and Basque Country. In Northern Ireland, a combination of economic disparities between the Catholic and Protestant populations, territorial division between the north and south of Ireland, and UK sovereignty over Northern Ireland led to competing nationalist demands and conflict. In the former Yugoslavia, the break-up of the Communist state led to a re-emergence of nationalist, ethnic and religious tensions, leading to a bitter civil war in the late 20th and early 21st centuries.

Activity 1

Write down the nation you consider to be your 'home'.

Discussion

Answering this question may appear self-evident and easy, but it involves making a set of personal and political decisions in order to identify which nation you feel most attached to. These decisions can be both politically significant and controversial.

For example, Daniel, co-author of this chapter, was born in Wales, but spent most of his childhood in England and a significant part of his adult life in South Africa. Which nation he calls 'home' involves a number of personal decisions that have social and political significance. His mother was born in England but her family emigrated from Ireland to England; his father was born in Wales but last lived there when he was 18. His parents also lived in South Africa. He usually ticks the 'British' box on questionnaires, but could identify himself as Welsh, though he has no ongoing connection with Wales and often feels English. However, because of his research and biography, people occasionally assume he is South African. In South Africa, he could have chosen to adopt dual nationality and his British national identity corresponded with a much larger English-speaking white population in the country, some of whom remained very conscious of their British heritage.

Along with all other UK nationals, he could identify as European. That choice could politically be a statement of his commitment to the United Kingdom's membership of the European Union; alternatively, rejecting that label would also be a political statement. In Scotland, Wales, England and Northern Ireland, claiming and proclaiming national identity can be used as a form of political leverage and has fed into powerful movements arguing for specific forms of political settlement such as devolution within the UK or, for some, independence from the UK. In addition, these movements have sought to develop, preserve and celebrate national culture and be identified as distinct from British identity.

1.1   The nationalist politics of the postbox

How people identify themselves with a particular national 'home' and the political significance of these choices is more than a matter of personal and collective identities. There are many symbols and practices of nationalism, often taken for granted, in everyday life. Such symbols and practices of 'banal nationalism' (Billig, 1995) can meaningfully and also unconsciously symbolise 'home' and help to create collective national identity. They can also become divisive and focal points for nationalist protest against the state, indicating the inequality of power about whose 'home' it is. The study of symbols by social scientists is known as semiotics.

Activity 2

Take a look at Figure 5.1, a red postbox (or pillar box) used by the UK Royal Mail. It is a familiar sight in the UK. If you have never thought of this as something you associate with 'home' or 'Britishness', consider how often iconic images of red postboxes appear on tourist souvenirs to represent the UK.

Figure 5.1   UK Royal Mail red postbox

The postbox symbolises the legal authority of the British state, with either the crown or Royal cypher of the head of state (the monarch) depicted on the side. Yet it is this political symbolism that has led to nationalist conflict over postboxes. When Queen Elizabeth II (1926–) was crowned in 1952, postboxes began to be produced with the Royal cypher EIIR on the side. 'EIIR' became a focus for Scottish nationalists, who wanted to preserve a distinct Scottish identity and reclaim independence from the UK. They argued that Elizabeth could not claim to be Elizabeth II of Scotland, but was Elizabeth I of

Scotland. This is because Queen Elizabeth I (1558–1601) had been Queen of England, not of Scotland, which at that time was an independent state. Postboxes in Scotland were vandalised and even blown up. Although the British state had the legal right to style the Queen as Elizabeth II, the 'Pillar Box War', as it was dubbed by the media, led to the Post Office removing EIIR from the side of postboxes in Scotland and replacing it with the Scottish crown (see Figure 5.2).

Figure 5.2   The Scottish crown on a postbox

Figure 5.3   The first British imperial postbox in Africa, Cape Agulhas, South Africa

Although the red postbox seems to be associated with home and is considered an aspect of British identity, the presence of red postboxes across the world is a legacy of the British empire. British colonies, under the control of the British state, also had red postboxes with the Royal cypher. These can still be seen on streets in places from Australia to Canada, and from Singapore to South Africa (Figure 5.3).

These postboxes have also become sites of nationalist controversy and protest because they are symbols of British colonial rule. For example, when southern Ireland became the independent Republic of Ireland in 1922, its red postboxes were repainted from red to green, the colour of the Irish nationalist movement. The Royal cypher was not removed, but the Irish state insignia was put alongside it. In Northern Ireland, red postboxes have been painted green by Irish Republicans as a form of protest against British sovereignty over the territory of Northern Ireland (Figure 5.4). In Cyprus, red postboxes were painted yellow upon independence from the UK (see Figure 5.5) and in Malta, the British royal insignia were removed from postboxes by the independent Maltese government in the 1980s. So the familiar and seemingly anodyne object of the red postbox can be both a symbol of national 'home' and an object that symbolises British state power. It can be seen as a divisive and unwelcome symbol for nationalist groups who wish to contest and remove that power.

Figure 5.4   Irish Republicans paint postboxes green as a protest against British sovereignty in Northern Ireland in 2009

Figure 5.5   A yellow post-independence postbox in Cyprus

Activity 3

Note down two or three national or nationalist symbols you have in your home or can regularly see in your community. Do you consciously think about them? What personal and political responses do you have to them?

Discussion

For Matt, co-author of this chapter, one obvious symbol is a British passport. Matt feels British, identifying with this symbol and the opportunities that having a British passport provides. Matt lives in London, so he uses the tube regularly and the London transport system is a very easily identifiable symbol of home. Matt enjoys going to the pub for a pint of bitter with his friends. The pub or bar is perhaps a clichéd symbol of Britain and Ireland – celebrated in popular culture on TV and on postcards. Although the pub is in decline, it still holds an important place within the collective consciousness of large parts of the British and Irish publics.

Summary

- The positioning and use of symbols can have a key role in emphasising particular nationalisms and denying others.

- Symbols are often the focus points of conflicts within the state between different nationalisms.

- The study of the role and use of symbols in society by social scientists is known as semiotics.

2   Nations and the state

The discussion of how people identify with one or more nations as a home, and how everyday objects such as postboxes can symbolise that nation and be a focus for nationalist protest, shows that issues of nationalism, belonging and homeland are complicated. The history of the modern world can, from some perspectives, be considered that of a history of different nations. In organisational and political terms, it is the state that people, as citizens, are formally linked to. However, there are international or transnational bodies that sit above the nation state, such as the European Union (EU) or the United Nations (UN). These are actually organisations of independent states. One of the founding principles of the UN is that states have **sovereign equality**, which as Bromley (2009, p. 409) says, 'refers to a situation in which each state recognises the legitimacy of others to govern and represent their territories and populations as far as international order is concerned'. The number of states in the UN increased from 51 in 1949 to 193 in 2014.

The nation state is broadly defined as a state in which there is a clear equivalence between the borders and character of the political unit or state and the cultural/national community within it. Yet many, if not most, nation states include groups who feel they are not part of the dominant national grouping and culture. One of the problems with many nation states is that they act on the basis that these groups do not exist and that their population is in fact one nation. Different national groupings within a state can require specific political considerations in order to feel part of it, so that competing nationalisms do not become the focus of political and sometimes violent conflict. In the UK context, some within the nationalist community in Northern Ireland would fit this definition of not feeling part of the UK nation state.

2.1   Defining the state

The state is one of the primary focuses for social science research. You will have seen in previous chapters how the state plays a key role in regulating people's lives, creating the conditions for the ownership of homes (or otherwise) and defining borders and the means to cross them. The state is the dominant form of political organisation on the world's landmass. It is the political 'home' to which all of us belong in

Sovereign equality
A formal notion that refers to the equal treatment of each state under international law. It does not mean that all states are equal in substance; for example, some states are richer or more powerful than others.

formal and legal terms. People are subject to its rules and requirements, must pay tax according to those rules and can be sanctioned and punished by the state if they break the law. These rules, regulations and responsibilities make up citizenship. Ultimately, the state claims not just the capacity but the right to employ force. The social and political theorist Max Weber defined the state as 'a human community that (successfully) claims the monopoly of the legitimate use of physical force within a given territory' (Weber, 1970, p. 78). The state can raise armies and direct them to fight external enemies as well as deploy them against threats from within a state's territory. When the state's monopoly of legitimate force is threatened, as in a civil war, its very existence is at threat. As long as the conflict continues, there is no legitimate authority.

The state is a political community formed by a territorial population and subject to one government. The distinction between state and government is that the state includes all the institutions and personnel, such as civil servants and military, while governments come and go, according to democratic processes where these are in place. The difference between state and government is symbolised by having a ceremonial president or monarch who is the head of state, and a prime minister who directs political matters and is the head of government. Yet there are multiple exceptions to these definitions: for example, overseas territories such as Gibraltar and New Caledonia are ultimately subject to the sovereignty, rules and regulations of the British and French states respectively.

Many states are divided in ways that grant sub-state entities varying levels of autonomy, such as the Special Administrative Region of Hong Kong, which has autonomous powers from China. The United States is an example of a federation, in which the individual states are partially self-governing. Regional powers are devolved in places such as Catalonia and the Basque Country in Spain, and Iraqi Kurdistan in Iraq.

The state shapes both everyday practices and societal interactions in a wide range of ways. Its reach extends far beyond the formal political institutions such as parliaments and beyond the government-run services such as state schools, hospitals, prisons, border controls, social security offices, tax inspectors, pensions, nationalised industries and public transport. Key aspects of human existence are enabled and regulated by the state: the right to marry is sanctioned by the state; the age at which it is legally permissible to smoke tobacco, drink alcohol and have sex is defined and policed by the state; the registration of all births and deaths is required by the state; and the state defines certain acceptable and unacceptable behaviours in family life – for example, defining what constitutes child abuse and having the power to take children into the care of the state.

The relationship people have with the state is heavily influenced by many factors, including the political system. Everyday life is quite different in a democracy from in an authoritarian non-democracy; there will be differences in the nature of the state's policies and laws between different democratically elected governments. So the extent to which people feel they 'belong' to and live in a territory that is their home and homeland is something that can be made or constructed by the state.

2.2   Creating a new 'rainbow nation' in the state of South Africa

One example of a state that has attempted to embrace competing and conflictual 'nations' to legitimise itself by making a 'homeland' for all its citizens is the Republic of South Africa. During the transition to democracy in the 1990s, one of the key aims of Nelson Mandela and the African National Congress (ANC) was to create a state and nation that could include all racial groups, reconcile former enemies and build national symbols that united this diverse country: a 'rainbow nation'. This involved a range of competing priorities. One was to include and accommodate the majority black population whose expectation in the context of a democratically elected government was to achieve parity over time with other communities within South Africa. Another priority was to reassure the white community because, as the South African academic Melissa Steyn has written, many in that community struggled to feel 'at home' during the transition as they found it difficult to understand and accept their loss of race-based privilege: 'There is an acute sense of loss of the familiar' following the end of apartheid, 'a loss of certainty, loss of comfort, loss of privilege, loss of well-known roles, a delusional home now collapsed' (Steyn, 2001, p. 150). The new government's national project to establish a new nation that would be a homeland for all involved the creation of unifying national symbols and images as part of a process of legitimising the new state. This section goes on to explore how these symbols and everyday images are political and can become symbols of home or of alienation.

National flags are key markers of national identity and not only symbolise but also generate nationalist feelings. Inevitably, they reflect the history and identity of a nation and state, and they can become contentious political symbols. This is apparent in the histories of the two flags of South Africa (see Figures 5.6 and 5.7). Figure 5.6 was the flag of South Africa between 1928 and 1994. It became a notorious symbol of apartheid South Africa. That flag was itself an attempt to reconcile and represent the different groups within the white population and overcome their fraught histories. The colours of orange, white and blue were drawn from the Dutch flag and symbolised the first Dutch settlers to the country in the 17th century. The three flags in the centre represent British colonial control of South Africa and the former Afrikaner (the descendants of the first Dutch settlers) republics of the Orange Free State and the South African Republic. In the late 19th century, there had been a war between the British and the Afrikaners (the Boer War) resulting in the defeat of the Afrikaner republics and the amalgamation of the Boer republics into a united South Africa in the British Empire. The humiliation of this defeat led to growing nationalist feeling in the Afrikaner community and demands for a new national flag to be designed, one that visually asserted the rights of Afrikaners in South Africa and to contest and remove British influence and control. When the (Afrikaner) National Party won office in the 1920s, they set about creating a new flag and Figure 5.6 clearly indicates that Afrikaner identity was more important in the flag than British identity, although British involvement in the country's history and politics was acknowledged. Black South Africans are not represented at all in this flag, reflecting their marginalisation.

Unsurprisingly, designing a new flag was one of the prime tasks during the transition from white minority rule to multiracial democracy after Nelson Mandela was released from prison in 1990. One of the key figures in the anti-apartheid movement, Mandela had been in prison since 1962 for crimes against the apartheid regime in South Africa. As the first democratic elections approached, the State Herald (the official responsible for all symbols and regalia for South Africa) was asked to design a flag that reflected the country's history and its different groups. Figure 5.7 shows the new flag that was unveiled in 1994 with green, gold and black, the colours of the ANC, the political party that had been banned for much of the apartheid period and that

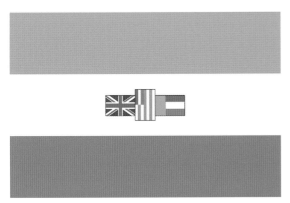

Figure 5.6   The flag of South Africa between 1928 and 1994

represented the views and demands of the black majority for a non-racist, democratic state. The colours blue and red symbolised both the colours of the British Union flag and the colours of the Afrikaner South African Republic and the Dutch tricolour flag. The flag therefore continued to symbolise the history of the country and draw from elements of the old flag. The black and white colours in the flag symbolise the main population groups in the country and that the new democracy would be a home to all racial groups.

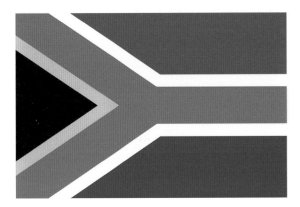

Figure 5.7   The new flag of South Africa unveiled in 1994

The new flag has proved to be a popular national symbol, ubiquitous across the country and among South Africans across the world. It is displayed at sports matches, on products and on the national airline (Figure 5.8), for example. Yet the old flag also sometimes appears at sporting matches and in certain communities. Its display remains politically provocative and offensive to many – symbolising a state that excluded the majority of the population on racial grounds. The display of the old flag has been interpreted as a sign of some white South

Africans' alienation from, and hostility towards, the new non-racial South African state. The new South African flag, like the old one, sought to help to create and symbolise a new South African nation, albeit one that would be inclusive and a home to all its racial and ethnic groups.

Figure 5.8 The South African flag incorporated in the livery of South African Airways

Like flags, national anthems can provoke strong awareness of national feelings, belonging and patriotism. However, the national anthem can also become politically controversial. Spain's national anthem, the 'Marcha Real', for example, has no lyrics in it. It is therefore not possible to sing it (officially at least). There are two main reasons for this. First, the lyrics the anthem once had were associated with the fascist regime of General Franco and were abandoned after the country became a democracy in the 1970s. Second, new lyrics were not written because there are regional and linguistic divides in Spain, namely the Basque, Catalan and Galician groups who have their own unofficial 'national anthems'. The Spanish state has yet to force or negotiate a politically acceptable set of lyrics.

Table 5.1   The National Anthem of South Africa, 1997

Verse	Language	Lyrics	English translation
1	Xhosa	Nkosi sikelel' iAfrika Maluphakanyisw' uphondo lwayo,	God bless Africa Let its (Africa's) horn be raised,
1	Zulu	Yizwa imithandazo yethu, Nkosi sikelela, thina lusapho lwayo.	Listen also to our prayers, Lord bless us, we are the family of it (Africa).
2	Sesotho	Morena boloka setjhaba sa heso, O fedise dintwa le matshwenyeho, O se boloke, O se boloke setjhaba sa heso, Setjhaba sa, South Afrika — South Afrika.	Lord bless our nation, Stop wars and sufferings, Save it, save our nation, The nation of South Africa – South Africa.
3	Afrikaans	Uit die blou van onse hemel, Uit die diepte van ons see, Oor ons ewige gebergtes, Waar die kranse antwoord gee.	Out of the blue of our heavens, Out of the depths of our seas, Over our everlasting mountains, Where the echoing crags resound.
4	English	Sounds the call to come together, And united we shall stand, Let us live and strive for freedom, In South Africa our land.	

In South Africa, the anthem, like the flag, has been the focus of political contestation and compromise. When South Africa was a colony, its anthem was the British national anthem. The growth of Afrikaner nationalism and the National Party winning office meant the replacement of this anthem with one that reflected Afrikaner history. The music and lyrics were thus replaced with 'Die Stem van Suid Afrika ('The Call of South Africa') which was sung in the Afrikaans language. In 1994, the new government was faced with a dilemma of what to replace this anthem with. The African National Congress had its own official anthem, a 19th-century hymn called 'Nkosi Sikelel' iAfrika' ('Lord Bless Africa'), which was sung at party and protest meetings from the 1920s onwards. As with the country's new flag, President Mandela decided to compromise. Both 'Die Stem van Suid Afrika' and 'Nkosi Sikelel' iAfrika' became official national anthems in 1994, but these two anthems were shortened and incorporated into a new anthem in 1997. Titled 'Nkosi Sikelel' iAfrika', the first and second verses and music are from the ANC's anthem, but are sung in three of the official languages of South Africa rather than just in Xhosa. The third verse is from 'Die Stem', as is the music, and is sung in Afrikaans. The final verse, sung in English, was written to express the new nation's desire to be inclusive and democratic. The new national anthem seeks to convey the political nature of the South African state. If you look at Table 5.1, you can see that its different verses reflect the different racial, ethnic and linguistic groups in the country and its different components are a focus of deeply held political and emotional feeling.

Activity 4

In Section 1, you read about the meaning and use of symbols to include or exclude citizens from having a sense of homeland. Why do you think symbols (such as flags, anthems, stamps and coins) express belonging to a nation or homeland? Are there any symbols that make you feel part of, or separate from, a homeland?

Discussion

For Matt, the union flag symbolises his Britishness, although he is conscious that the flag only represents three of the four parts of the United Kingdom (England, Scotland and Northern Ireland). The representation of Northern Ireland is problematic because St Patrick's saltire is meant to represent the whole of Ireland, not Northern Ireland, but has continued to be on the Union flag despite Eire becoming a separate state. There is no Welsh representation on the Union flag because, when the flag was created in the early 19th century, Wales was deemed to be part of England and represented by the flag of St George.

The anthem of the UK is 'God Save the Queen' (or 'God Save the King' if there is a male monarch). Broadly speaking, Matt is happy with a limited and constitutionally embedded monarchy, but would prefer the words of the national anthem for the UK to be more focused on its citizens than its head of state.

The national flag and anthem are common symbols of a nation, but even the money of a nation state expresses national identification. Coins, bank notes and stamps symbolise the nation and can become politically controversial if certain groups in society feel under- or misrepresented. In the UK, the currency has sought to embrace and accommodate the different national groups, such as the national plants or emblems of England, Wales, Scotland and Northern Ireland, with overall British sovereignty symbolised by the Queen on bank notes and coins. In the attachment to these symbols you might also see the connection here with the desire by some in the UK to retain the pound rather than adopt the Euro.

Figure 5.9   The notes and coins of South Africa during apartheid

Returning to the example of South Africa, the country's currency has been the Rand since 1961. During apartheid, the national symbols on the currency were the protea flower, the springbok deer and Jan van Riebeeck, the Dutch colonial official who led the first settlement of Europeans to the country in the 17th century (see Figure 5.9), forming a key part of Afrikaner claims to control South Africa. In 1994, van Riebeeck was removed from notes and replaced with politically neutral animals and industrial symbols, while coins were gradually replaced with ones showing the new national coat of arms (see Figure 5.10).

Figure 5.10   The coins of South Africa's multiracial democracy

The patriotic display of nationalist symbols, such as flags or wearing national colours, is also evident during international sporting events. Such events and resulting emotions are important in generating and sustaining national feeling and belonging to a 'home'. In 1995, the newly democratic South Africa hosted the rugby World Cup. Sport itself is a source of inequality and rugby had been a game primarily associated with white Afrikaners. One of the most pictured moments from that World Cup is when President Mandela handed the cup to Francois Pienaar, captain of the South African national rugby team, while wearing the green and orange Springbok jersey (Figure 5.11). Many commentators considered it to be a defining moment of 'nation building' in the new country. The picture of Mandela and Pienaar points to the symbolic overcoming of bitter nationalist divisions based on ethnicity, history and politics (Imray, 2013).

In 2010, South Africa hosted the FIFA football World Cup, the first African country to do so. Football has traditionally had a much larger following in the country's black community than in the white population, who had played and supported rugby and cricket more widely. It was striking, however, how the matches and celebrations outside stadiums included South Africans of all racial groups. The South Africans' successful hosting of the FIFA World Cup was a source of great national pride in the country and further proof of the successful process of building a new nation, albeit one still heavily unequal along racial lines.

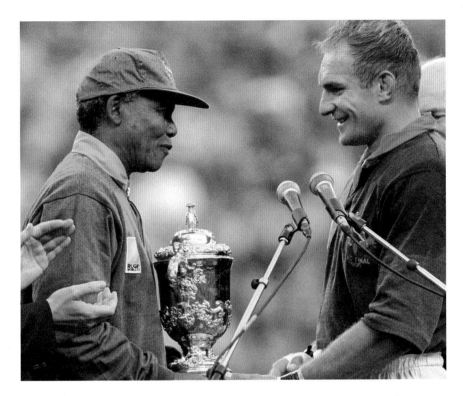

Figure 5.11 Nelson Mandela and Francois Pienaar, Rugby World Cup, 1995

During this process of transformation in South Africa, as it moved from being an apartheid state to a multi-ethnic nation, much of the work that went on in civil society and the political process was accomplished by South Africans. However, the transformative process was not an internal one alone, and external pressures were brought to bear to achieve specific aims. These pressures were at different levels, from global social movements boycotting South African products, and countries bordering South Africa offering military support to ANC guerrillas, to international bodies such as the UN opposing apartheid. The racial inequality on which the white South African state was based was widely opposed internationally.

However, not all nationalist demands for a homeland are as successful. The processes by which individual national groups and nations are able to successfully make claims to a political role within a state, create a state of their own, or even express a cultural or political identity within a homeland, are uneven and unequal. They are subject to wider interests and power relationships within the international system and point to the role of power and inequality in who can successfully achieve nationhood. This will be explored further in Section 3, focusing on the case of the Kurds.

Summary

- States are often the sites of conflict between different groups who make claims for the state as their homeland.

- Symbols, images and rituals can become the focus for tensions and conflicts that arise from these competing claims.

- Symbols and practices can be a source of either political and cultural alienation or integration, depending on the way they are created and used within a state.

3   Are all nation claims equal?

For political scientists, there are tensions at play in the international arena between the principle of sovereignty (the rights of states to claim jurisdiction over their own citizens) and the rights of groups within states to separate and form their own 'states'.

When a group claims to be a nation, it also identifies and lays claim to a 'homeland' and territory. The right of national self-determination is the right of people to possess their own government, democratic or otherwise. Therefore, nationalist movements seek political recognition as well as political independence for their homeland. This assertion of self-determination, or self-rule, gives the nation its political character and nationalism its political drive.

The principle of national self-determination was formally expressed in international politics by the Atlantic Charter of 1941, which was a joint statement between British Prime Minister Winston Churchill and US President Franklin D. Roosevelt. That right was reaffirmed by the UN Covenant on Civil and Political Rights, which stated, 'All peoples have the right to self-determination. By virtue of that right they freely determine their political status and pursue their economic, social and cultural rights' (OHCHR, 1966).

This statement, and the movement of history since it was first made, have given impetus to a wide range of nationalist movements across Africa and Asia, which protested and fought against European colonial rule in a series of both peaceful and violent campaigns that led to the creation of many new states including India, Kenya and Vietnam. **Decolonisation** was broadly accepted by the wider international community, if not by the colonial powers themselves, and it is a good example of how in many cases the principle of self-determination has been emphasised over the principle of sovereignty.

Many nations have been constructed in the course of recent struggles. The anti-colonial/independence movements in Africa and Asia that demanded national self-determination can be viewed as modern examples of nationalism in their political demands and by the international support and acceptance of those demands. Imperial powers sometimes fostered nationalist divisions and feeling in order to increase their colonial power. But nationalist feeling in colonies could also be fostered by the very existence of colonial rule, which created a

Decolonisation
The process by which imperial states withdraw from colonial territories and those territories re-emphasise the centrality of their original national territory/state. Characterised by both peaceful and violent transition, the concept is associated primarily with the retreat from empire of the European powers such as France, Britain, Spain, Portugal and the Netherlands in the decades following the Second World War.

sense of common purpose and political demands against that rule. The same could be argued about the nationalist movements in much of eastern Europe, in countries such as Poland and Czechoslovakia where nationalist feeling and demands for autonomy and self-rule were fostered in the face of authoritarian, communist (and, by implication, foreign and Soviet) rule.

As noted earlier, nations are viewed as emerging out of history, with common stories, traditions and national events that are celebrated or mourned. To what extent, though, is this history invented, manipulated or obscured to suit the politics of the moment or by a framework of international institutions?

There are two different viewpoints within political science, or more specifically international studies, that divide opinion about the way the international system works in practice. One is the liberal approach; the other is the realist approach.

3.1   Liberalism versus realism

Civil society
The ways in which the interests and views of society are represented and expressed through the involvement of individual citizens, groups and organisations. Participation in civil society includes interest groups such as sports clubs, the Scouts and Guides, religious and faith-based organisations, and non-governmental organisations such as trade unions, charities and campaign groups. In South Africa, religious groups and trade unions were both active in the anti-apartheid campaign.

A liberal view is one that sees international order working through a set of agreed rules and principles, embodied through the UN organisation, which governs how states act towards each other and how they govern their own citizens. The view enshrines the principle of sovereignty. It has its origins in idealism, the idea that people and the states that they form have no interest in, and little to gain from, warfare, and more to gain from working together. It argues that, while states pursue their own interests, these are best and most rationally achieved through cooperation rather than conflict.

Liberal theorists would also argue that the state is part of a wider international system that includes non-governmental organisations (NGOs) and sub-state-based actors within a wider global **civil society**. Moravscik (2011) argues that international institutions can improve domestic democratic processes by opening them up to international scrutiny.

Liberal theorists believe in the equality of states as an ideal. However, there is a recognition that, in reality, some states are more equal than others (as witnessed by the role and function of the Security Council at the UN) and that bigger states can work in the interests of others as well as themselves.

In contrast, the realist view of how states interact is based on the idea that there is no legitimate authority internationally and that international order is based on the **balance of power** rather than the governance of the UN. Realists see the attempt to mitigate the possible conflicts and tensions between states through the establishment of international institutions as flawed because these are fundamentally weak structures; states will not give up their sovereignty to such bodies. From a realist point of view, states are primarily self-interested. Realists view the state as the primary structure and the pursuit of national interest and power as the primary force driving politics in the international system. This can be political power, but invariably political power is backed up by military and economic reality.

Two key principles underline the realist perspective. The first is that the international system is characterised by a state of anarchy. In international relations, anarchy does not refer to disorder or chaos but rather to the absence of legitimate authority. An international anarchy may or may not offer a sense of order globally, depending on the balance of power at any given time (Bromley, 2009). The second principle, emphasised by the theorist Waltz (1979), is that, as each state tries to maximise its own strategic and military position, a balance of power in the international system emerges, with states shifting alliances and increasing military spending to nullify the strategic advantages of other competitor states.

Balance of power
The principle by which states, fearing the potential threat of other states' military and strategic capabilities, ensure their security by aligning with one another to counteract the power of the strongest or most threatening.

3.2   The Kurds: applying liberal and realist perspectives

A good example through which to view the complexities of the international system and the ability of some nations and states to influence, support or deny the claims of others is the case of the Kurds. The Kurds number between 25 and 30 million people and have been recognised as a distinct ethnicity and nation within the UN and by many governments. They represent the largest ethnic group in the world that does not have its own nation state, Kurdistan. The Kurdish nation's claims to statehood and the likelihood of it being achieved are reflective of wider international circumstances and the relationships between other nations and states, and can be approached from both a liberal and a realist perspective.

The homeland of the Kurdish people, which many Kurds would see as the basis for a Kurdish state, straddles the borders of four other states:

Syria, Iraq, Turkey and Iran (see Figure 5.12). As Ignatieff (1995, p. 136) says, 'It has been the Kurds' misfortune that their homeland is the meeting point of four of the most aggressive and expansionary nationalisms in the modern world: two Arabic, one Turkish and one Iranian'.

Following the First World War, the Ottoman Empire, which had sided with Germany and the Austro-Hungarian Empire and had lost the war, was subject to a process of dismemberment. US President Woodrow Wilson's principle of the 'self-determination of peoples' coincided with the desire of the other victors (the UK, France and Italy) to break up the Ottoman Empire into units more reflective of its constituent peoples, while replacing Ottoman influence over the wider Middle East with their own. The 1920 Treaty of Sèvres reflected this in its identification of a Kurdish state taken from areas of the Ottoman Empire but excluding territory and Kurdish populations in Syria, Iraq and Iran.

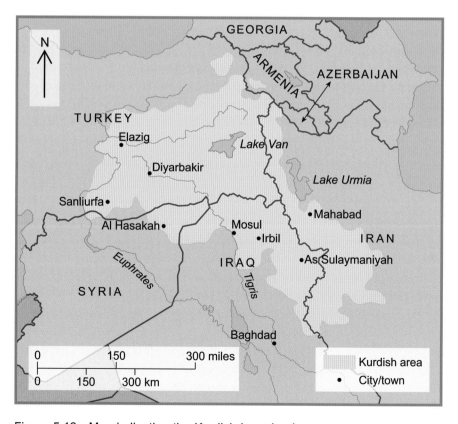

Figure 5.12 Map indicating the Kurdish homeland

This process highlights the role by what were then the European colonial powers in deciding the shape and populations of specific states and in the creation of nations. The existence of many of the current members of the UN (and the non-existence or recognition of many nations and ethnic groups) can be traced back in part or wholly to the decisions taken by European administrators in the 18th, 19th and early 20th centuries in drawing lines on maps.

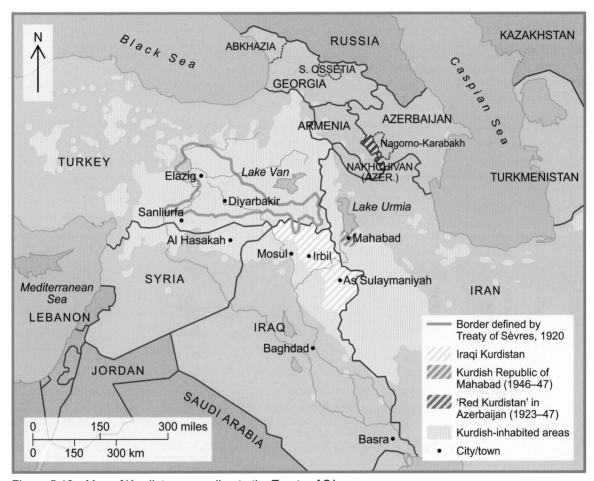

Figure 5.13   Map of Kurdistan according to the Treaty of Sèvres

However, Kurdistan, as outlined in Figure 5.13, did not emerge as an independent state. A combination of resurgent Turkish nationalism, a new US president with different foreign policy priorities, and an inability of states granted parts of the Ottoman Empire to defend them led to different de facto arrangements. Ultimately, the treaty of

Lausanne in 1923 led to the Kurdish nation and state being subsumed back within the Turkish state.

During the remainder of the 20th century and into the 21st century, Kurdish claims to nationhood have depended on the international situation. In all four states in which there are large Kurdish populations, the ability of Kurdish groups to actively participate in civil society as Kurds has been actively discriminated against (Özkirimli, 2013, p. 2). In Turkey, the Kurdish identity was not recognised under military rule, which ended in 1983, the government defining Kurds as 'Mountain Turks'. Forced **assimilation** has left many Turkish Kurds unable to speak their own language; speaking Kurdish was only recently deemed acceptable in the Turkish Parliament, and until 2002 its use was not allowed in the media. Only in 2009 was a television channel broadcasting in Kurdish allowed and the right to choose Kurdish as an elective subject in Turkish schools made possible (Derince, 2013, p. 5). In Syria, many of the ethnic Kurdish population were denied Syrian citizenship rights until 2012/13, and thus were unable to exit Syria legitimately. In Iran there are significant restrictions on the ability of Kurds to express themselves politically and culturally. In Iraq, a process of Arabisation forced large Kurdish populations out of their traditional homelands in the north of the country and culminated in the large-scale killing of thousands of Kurds at Halabja in Northern Iraq in 1989, which led to the imposition of a no-fly zone in Northern Iraq by the Western powers of France, the UK and the United States.

Those arguing from the realist perspective might contend that Kurdish aspirations for political autonomy or even statehood have been subsumed to greater strategic considerations of other states. Turkey's strategic geography adjacent to the then Soviet Union and its status as the only member of the North Atlantic Treaty Organisation (NATO) in the Middle East took priority for other NATO members over supporting minority rights, such as those of the Kurds. Likewise, the Soviet Union and its successor state, the Russian Federation, has actively cultivated the Syrian state for similar geopolitical reasons, with Syria providing the Russians with a strategic presence on the Mediterranean through the acceptance of a Russian naval base at Tartus on the Syrian coast. In Iran the emergence of the Islamic Republic following the 1979 revolution saw any Western influence over minority rights curtailed, with the Western powers actively and covertly backing Saddam Hussein in the Gulf War against Iran and turning a

Assimilation
The process by which minority groups take on the cultural and linguistic characteristics of the dominant group – for example, Kurds in Turkey learning to speak Turkish rather than Kurdish. The process may be subject to coercive pressure or be passive in nature.

blind eye to the issue of Kurdish oppression and discrimination in Iraq as a consequence. The West only turned against Saddam Hussein's Ba'athist regime following the latter's invasion of the oil-rich state of Kuwait in 1991.

Realists might also point to the emergence of the Kurds in Iraq as potential allies of the West against resurgent Islamic extremism since the invasion of Iraq, with the fragility of a post-war Iraqi government enabling a stable Kurdistan autonomous region to emerge. This changing context suggests that a nascent Kurdish state and claims for independence are increasingly being seen as legitimate. The Syrian conflict that began in 2011, and the de facto independence of Kurdish areas in the north-east of Syria, whose borders connect it to Iraqi Kurdistan, again suggest possible conditions for a re-emergent set of claims for a Kurdish homeland. Rapprochement between the Turkish government and its Kurdish population since 2009 can also be seen in this context, as Turkey reflects the wider Western perception of the Kurdish nation as possible allies in the Middle East. The other complicating issue is that all the countries in which the Kurds are minorities fought their own nationalist struggles to free themselves from colonial or quasi-colonial arrangements; this makes the criticisms by what were once colonial powers of the treatment of minorities look like **neocolonialism.**

Neocolonialism
The informal dominance of one country over another, the latter often once a colony of the former. It may be expressed through both overt and subtle forms of political influence, economic control and cultural imperialism.

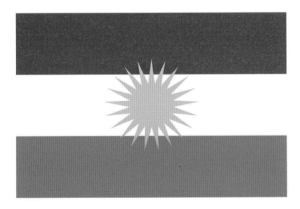

Figure 5.14   The Kurdistan flag

Those from a liberal perspective might argue that this articulation of the rights of sovereign states is legitimate. It is an argument that has been used effectively in the UN in supporting the sovereignty of states where the construction of post-colonial states has itself led to the emergence of new national minorities and claims to nationhood.

Sub-state actors
Organisations that operate beneath or alongside states and seek to influence or change events in the international system. They can range from non-governmental organisations (NGOs) to multinational corporations, religious groups, armed organisations such as al-Qaeda or ETA, or overseas communities such as the Armenian or Jewish diasporas.

Likewise, the petitioning of the UN by various governments and international agencies to establish Kurdish autonomy supports the liberal approach to negotiating the tensions between principles of state sovereignty and the right to self-determination for 'nations' and 'homelands' through discussion and debate in the international arena. Liberals would acknowledge that this process has been long drawn out, but has achieved tangible benefits for the Kurdish community in Turkey and in Iraq through the involvement of international organisations as well as **sub-state actors**.

Summary

- In the desire for some nations to have homelands of their own there is a tension between the right of self-determination for nations and that of the sovereignty of existing states.

- The liberal and realist positions are two contrasting approaches among a wider number used in international studies to explain how the international system works.

- In the specific context of the chapter, these approaches can offer different perspectives on how aspirations for a homeland or legitimation of minority rights within a state, and the conflicts that result, are dealt with in the international system.

Conclusion

The beginning of this chapter asked you to think about what constitutes 'home' in political and international terms. The first part of the chapter explored the different interpretations of nationalism, from those that consider it to be 'imagined' and subject to change to those that believe it is deeply rooted in history and passed down the generations. The chapter then explored the idea of the state and how the state lays claim to providing home for the majority of the world's people. The state is an important institutional and political embodiment of home, framing policies, choosing symbols and setting practices that define the terms of inclusion and exclusion for individuals and groups. The state makes laws, raises taxes and armies, and regulates most aspects of everyday life. Yet it is actually the nation that people feel belonging to and, in many circumstances, the nation and state are not one and the same. One state – the UK, for example – can contain several nations.

In everyday terms nationalism is expressed in symbols, rituals and celebrations. These symbols can become politically controversial should groups within society contest the state's legitimacy and sovereignty, as you saw with postboxes. When a new political order emerges, such as in South Africa, the redesign of national symbols is an important process of making a political homeland.

The other main example explored in this chapter was that of the Kurdish people. Their national claim to recognition within various states, or even to full self-determination, has not been met, due in part to wider geo-political issues.

The desire by nations within states for self-determination is a defining political movement in modern history. The claims of different groups to self-determine a national 'home' and the competing claims of state sovereignty continue to drive global politics and create both peaceful and violent political demands.

References

Anderson, B. (1983) *Imagined Communities: Reflections on the Origins and Spread of Nationalism*, London, Verso.

Billig, M. (1995) *Banal Nationalism*, London, Sage.

Bromley, S. (2009) 'Pirates and predators: authority and power in international affairs', in Bromley, S., Clarke, J., Hinchliffe, S. and Taylor, S. (eds) *Exploring Social Lives*, Milton Keynes, The Open University.

Derince, M. (2013) 'A break or continuity? Turkey's politics of Kurdish language in the new millennium', *Dialectical Anthropology*, vol. 37, no. 1, p. 5.

Gellner, E. (1983) *Nations and Nationalism,* Ithaca, NY, Cornell University Press.

Hobsbawm, E. (1983) *The Invention of Tradition*, Cambridge, Cambridge University Press.

Ignatieff, M. (1993) *Blood and Belonging*, London, BBC Books/Chatto & Windus.

Imray, G. (2013) '1995 World Cup final put Nelson Mandela's belief in the power of sports on display', *Huffington Post* [Online]. Available at www.huffingtonpost.com/2013/12/05/rugby-world-cup-nelson-mandela-sports_n_4394712.html (Accessed 11 November 2014).

Moravscik, A. (2011) 'Affirming democracy in international organisations', in Goldstein, J. and Pevehouse, J. (eds) *International Relations*, London, Longman Press.

Office of the High Commissioner for Human Rights (OHCHR) (1966) *International Covenant on Civil and Political Rights* [Online]. Available at www.ohchr.org/en/professionalinterest/pages/ccpr.aspx (Accessed 11 November 2014).

Özkirimli, U. (2014) 'Multiculturalism, recognition and the "Kurdish question" in Turkey: the outline of a normative framework', *Democratization*, vol. 21, no. 6, p. 2.

Smith, A. (1995) *Nations and Nationalism in a Global Era*, Cambridge, Polity.

Steyn, M. (2001) *Whiteness Just Isn't What it Used to Be: White Identity in a Changing South Africa*, Albany, NY, State University of New York Press.

Waltz, K. (1979) *Theory of International Politics*, Reading, MA, Addison-Wesley.

Weber, M. (1970) *From Max Weber: Essays in Sociology*, London, Routledge.

Acknowledgements

Every effort has been made to contact copyright holders. If any have been inadvertently overlooked the publishers will be pleased to make the necessary arrangements at the first opportunity.

Grateful acknowledgement is made to the following sources:

Chapter 1: *Table 1.1*: From Silva, E. (2010) *Technology, Culture, Family: Influences on Home Life*, Palgrave Macmillan, © Elizabeth B. Silva; *Figure 1.1*: © SSPL/Getty Images; *Figure 1.2*: Adapted from http://images.scholastic.co.uk/assets/a/c8/8e/je06-who-lives-in-a-house-268593.pdf; *Figure 1.4*: Adapted from Silva, E. (2010) *Technology, Culture, Family: Influences on Home Life*, Palgrave Macmillan, © Elizabeth B. Silva; *Figure 1.5*: © Hero Images Inc./Alamy; *Figure 1.6*: © Ian Shaw/Alamy.

Chapter 2: *Figure 2.1*: © Quentin Bargate/Dreamstime.com; *Figure 2.2*: © WiNG. This file is licensed under the Creative Commons Attribution-ShareAlike Licence http://creativecommons.org/licenses/by-sa/3.0/; *Figure 2.3*: © Kevin Walsh/Alamy; *Figure 2.4*: Adapted from http://chandigarh.gov.in/knowchd_map.htm; *Figure 2.6*: © Chaloner Woods/Stringer/Getty Images; *Figure 2.7*: © PF-(usna)/Alamy; *Figure 2.9*: © James Cheadle/Alamy; *Figure 2.10*: © Bloomberg/Getty Images; *Figure 2.11*: © Elmtree Images/Alamy; *Figure 2.12*: © iStockphoto.com/James Augustus.

Chapter 3: *Figure 3.2*: © Money Week www.moneyweek.com; *Figure 3.3*: Taken from www.nationwide.co.uk/about/house-price-index/download-data#xtab:uk-series; *Figure 3.4*: Andrews, D. and Caldera Sánchez, A. (2011), 'The evolution of homeownership rates in selected OECD countries: demographic and public policy influences', *OECD Journal: Economic Studies*, vol. 2011/1. http://dx.doi.org/10.1787/eco_studies-2011-5kg0vswqpmg2; *Table 3.5*: Taken from 'The wealth and savings of UK families on the eve of the crisis' © The Institute for Fiscal Studies.

Chapter 4: *Figure 4.4*: © Guardian News & Media Ltd; *Figure 4.5 left*: © B.G.D. This file is licensed under the Creative Commons Attribution-Noncommercial-ShareAlike Licence http://creativecommons.org/licenses/by-nc-sa/2.0/; *Figure 4.5 right*: © Ruben G. Herrera. This file is licensed under the Creative Commons Attribution-ShareAlike Licence http://creativecommons.org/licenses/

by-sa/2.0/; *Figure 4.6*: © Robert Harding Picture Library Ltd/Alamy; *Figure 4.7*: © Copyright Sasi Group (University of Sheffield) and Mark Newman (University of Michigan). This file is licensed under the Creative Commons Attribution-Noncommercial-NoDerivatives Licence http://creativecommons.org/licenses/by-nc-nd/3.0/; *Figure 4.8*: © Londonmapper Project. This file is licensed under the Creative Commons Attribution-Noncommercial-NoDerivatives Licence http://creativecommons.org/licenses/by-nc-nd/3.0/; *Figure 4.9*: © Dinodia Photos/Alamy; *Figure 4.10*: © Martin Godwin; *Figure 4.11*: © iStockphoto.com/fotoMonkee; *Figure 4.12*: © Kevin Harding/Alamy Images; *Figure 4.13*: © *Landscape with Jacob and Laban and Laban's Daughters*, 1654, Claude Lorrain (Claude Gellee) (1600–82)/Petworth House, Sussex, UK/Bridgeman Images; *Figure 4.14*: © *Monarch of the Glen*, 1851 (oil on canvas), Landseer, Sir Edwin (1802–73)/United Distillers and Vitners/Bridgeman Images; *Figure 4.15*: © Matthew Holley.

Chapter 5: *Figure 5.1*: © Jongleu100 via Wikipedia; *Figure 5.2*: © Kitmaster via Wikipedia; *Figure 5.3*: © Stefan Schafer. This file is licensed under the Creative Commons Attribution-ShareAlike Licence http://creativecommons.org/licenses/by-sa/3.0/; *Figure 5.4*: © Baldeadly via Wikipedia; *Figure 5.5*: © Christos Vittoratos. This file is licensed under the Creative Commons Attribution Licence http://creativecommons.org/licenses/by/3.0/; *Figure 5.6*: © Universal Images Group/Alamy; *Figure 5.7*: © iStockphoto.com/liangpv; *Figure 5.8*: © imageBROKER/Alamy; *Figure 5.9*: © NJR ZA. This file is licensed under the Creative Commons Attribution-ShareAlike Licence http://creativecommons.org/licenses/by-sa/3.0/; *Figure 5.10*: © iStockphoto.com/strizhakov; *Figure 5.11*: © Jean-Pierre Muller/Getty Images; *Figure 5.14*: © tony4urban/Shutterstock.

DD103 Module team

Academic team

Fiona Barnes, Associate Lecturer

Shonil Bhagwat, Lecturer in Geography

Jonathan Blundell, Associate Lecturer

Melissa Butcher, Senior Lecturer in Geography

Victoria Canning, Lecturer in Criminology

Daniel Conway, Lecturer in Politics and International Studies

Sue Cowley, Associate Lecturer

Deborah Drake, Senior Lecturer in Criminology (Deputy Module Team Chair)

Umut Erel, Lecturer in Sociology

Jessica Evans, Senior Lecturer in Cultural and Media Studies

Steve Garner, Senior Lecturer in Social Policy

Kim Hammond, Research Associate

Martin Holborn, Associate Lecturer

Janet Hunter, Associate Lecturer

Vicky Johnson, Associate Lecturer

Nikoleta Jones, Lecturer in Human Geography

Giles Mohan, Professor of International Development

Andy Morris, Staff Tutor (Deputy Module Team Chair)

Karim Murji, Senior Lecturer in Sociology (Module Team Chair)

Mel Nettle, Associate Lecturer

Stuart Parris, Senior Lecturer in Economics

Rob Parsons, Associate Lecturer

Rajiv Prabakhar, Lecturer in Personal Finance

George Revill, Senior Lecturer in Geography

Alan Shipman, Lecturer in Economics

Elizabeth Silva, Professor of Sociology

Roberto Simonetti, Head of Economics Department

Bradon Smith, Research Associate

Joe Smith, Senior Lecturer in Environment

Matt Staples, Staff Tutor

Andrew Trigg, Senior Lecturer in Economics

Dave Turner, Associate Lecturer

Edward Wastnidge, Lecturer in Politics and International Studies

Sophie Watson, Professor of Sociology

Katy Wheeler, Lecturer in Sociology

Teresa Willis, Associate Lecturer

External assessor

Professor Fran Tonkiss, London School of Economicsr

Production team

David Adamson, Curriculum Assistant

Roshni Amin, Sound and Vision Producer

Melanie Bayley, Media Project Manager

Wendy Chalmers, Learning and Teaching Librarian

Sian Contell, Sound and Vision Assistant

Nicholas Dragffy, Production Editor

Jane Fransella, Commissioner

Ryan Hayle, Interactive Media Developer

Paul Hillery, Graphics Media Developer

Matthew Holley, Sound and Vision Media Developer

Diane Hopwood, Licensing and Acquisitions Assistant

Gareth Hudson, Senior Project Manager

Jason Jarratt, Interactive Media Developer

Alex Keable-Crouch, Online Services Media Developer

Joanna Mack, Senior Sound and Vision Producer

Adam Nightingale, Digital Development Editor

Neil Paterson, Media Assistant

Eileen Potterton, Curriculum Manager

Lauren Robinson, Licensing and Acquisitions Assistant

Lindsey Smith, Digital Development Editor

Eddie Tunnah, Senior Careers and Employability Adviser

Howie Twiner, Graphics Media Developer

Laura Underwood, Digital Development Editor

Amanda Vaughan, Curriculum Assistant

Liz Vidler, Curriculum Manager

The module team would also like to thank the following freelance staff: Mandy Anton (cover design), Clare Butler (proofreader), Isobel McLean (indexer) and Nina Randall (book editor).

Video production

Jane Diblin, Series Producer, Angel Eye Media

Rosa Rodger and Morgan Phillips, Camera/Director, Angel Eye Media

Sam Piranty, Researcher, Angel Eye Media

Index